WISDOM
from the Proverbs

WISDOM

from the Proverbs

A 40-Day Devotional Journey

Peter Horrobin

Sovereign World

Published by
Sovereign World Ltd
PO Box 784
Ellel
Lancaster
LA1 9DA
United Kingdom

www.sovereignworld.com

Twitter: @sovereignworld
Facebook: www.facebook.com/sovereignworld

Published November 2018

ISBN
978-1-85240-831-2 (print)
978-1-85240-836-7 (epub)
978-1 85240-841-1-(kindle)

British Library Cataloguing-in-Publication Data
A catalogue record for this book is available from the British Library.

Typeset by Avocet Typeset, Somerton, Somerset, TA11 6RT
Printed in the UK by Bell and Bain Ltd, Glasgow

Contents

Contents

Introduction

WISDOM

Information and wisdom are very different! Someone could be the most knowledgeable person in the world but be seriously deficient in wisdom and have little understanding of what it means to live a godly life. And another person may be relatively unlearned, and yet be able to exercise profound wisdom in the decisions they have to make on life's journey.

It's not unusual to read the achievements of a very clever person, and then discover that their private life was an absolute disaster, punctuated with the consequences of unwise decisions, broken relationships and financial loss. And because bad news sells newspapers, the editors are never slow to profile the mistakes of the rich and famous.

Young people idolise the stars of the music, entertainment and sporting world. But the private lives of their heroes or heroines are rarely known for their godliness! Beneath the veneer of success and popularity can lie a maelstrom of sinful behaviour, activities and relationships. It's no surprise, therefore that, when they grow up, their lives replicate the behaviour of the people they follow.

When Solomon succeeded his father David to the throne of Israel, he went up to Gibeon and before the tabernacle he enquired of the Lord at the beginning of his reign. The Lord said to him, *"Ask for whatever you want me to give you"* (2 Chronicles 1:7). And because Solomon asked for knowledge and wisdom, and not riches and wealth, the Lord said he would give him both. Solomon became renowned for both his wisdom and his wealth, exceeding anything that had ever been known previously.

It is generally understood that the wisdom Solomon was blessed with was nothing less than the Spirit of God speaking through him. It was a gift of God. We also read about this gift of God in James 1:5 where it says, *"If any of you lacks wisdom, he should ask God, who gives generously to all without finding fault, and it will be given him."*

With the knowledge and wisdom that God had given him, Solomon's reign was extraordinarily successful. He prospered. And not only did he prosper but he was privileged with the task of building the temple that his father David had dreamt of. On a second occasion, when the temple was built, Solomon was blessed with another direct encounter with the Lord, who appeared to him at night and said, *"I have heard your prayer and have chosen this place for myself as a temple for sacrifices"* (2 Chronicles 7:12). And then God said in verse 14 *"If my people, who are called by my name, will humble themselves and pray and seek my face and turn from their wicked ways, then will I hear from heaven and will forgive their sin and heal their land."*

This is an extraordinary promise which is rich in meaning – both for the nation of Israel and God's people of all generations. For us now, as individuals, I have seen God's promise of healing and restoration, subsequent to humble repentance, fulfilled a thousand times over in the lives of people of all nations and cultures. God loves to honour His promises. Peter reminds his readers of this divine principle when he says, *"Humble yourselves, therefore, under God's mighty hand, that he may lift you up in due time"* (1 Peter 5:6).

Returning now to the book of Proverbs, within the confines of these 31 chapters God has placed the condensed wisdom that was received as a gift by Solomon. What Solomon wrote down in chapter after chapter of pithy, expressive, dynamic and challenging sayings is like a bottle of vitamin pills for the soul. But in order to know the blessing that God planned for His people through their use, we have to humble ourselves (that means deal with our pride) and let God speak to our heart.

In this 40-day Devotional, I have selected 40 of these sayings, which embody life-transforming spiritual principles, as a journey of spiritual understanding which will speak to the heart. But for the maximum blessing and benefit, the 'vitamin pills' have to be taken and I would encourage you to set out on this journey with an open heart towards the Lord, praying that He will speak into your life and bring healing and restoration to your soul as you take these forty steps, drawing on the Wisdom God placed within the Proverbs to build you up in Him.

How to use this book

This book has been laid out as a 40-step journey of faith. It was designed to be read little by little, one day at a time. Before you begin to read each day's Scripture and the devotional reading, I would encourage you to spend a few moments in prayer – lay aside all the concerns of the moment and ask the Holy Spirit to open up to you God's Word and to minister His truth into your inner being.

Then read the Scripture for the day – not once, but two or three times, allowing God to speak to you personally through the words from Scripture. Next, read the devotional with an open heart asking God to show you how the things that are said can relate to events and circumstances in your own life. You may find it helpful to read the devotional through again.

At the end of each devotional is a suggested prayer which will help you anchor the daily truths into the reality of your own life. But I would encourage you to pray more personally as well, applying whatever God has said to you through the devotional to your own situation.

Finally, there is a space for you to make your own personal comments about the Scripture and the devotional and keep a record of what God says to you. It has always been a huge encouragement to me to look back at the things that God has said or done in the past and track the record of God's hand on my life.

I pray that this little book will be a rich blessing to you and that as you move on with God you will know His presence and empowering day by day.

Day 1 — 1/2/19

On What are You Leaning?

"Trust in the Lord with all your heart and lean not unto your own understanding. In all your ways acknowledge him, and he will make your paths straight." Proverbs 3:5-6

The leaning tower of Pisa, in Italy, is very unstable. When people first see the structure they are amazed that it is still standing! Massive amounts of careful engineering work have been necessary to preserve this iconic structure which attracts tourists from all over the world. It is a massive money earner for Italy.

But it is not what the architect intended! It was meant to be upright. It leans because the ground on which it is built was too soft on one side of the structure. It is quite literally

13

leaning according to its own understanding of weight, pressure and gravity!

If the ground on which we build our lives is not firm, then we, too, will lean according to our own understanding and go our own way. It is absolutely vital that we follow the advice of our Scripture for today and *'Trust in the Lord'*. Only He knows everything about us and our circumstances and only He is able to direct our steps according to His plans and purposes for our lives.

This is how our devotional journey should begin – by humbling ourselves and choosing to trust that God's Word and His teaching is more important and much more reliable than our own ideas and inclinations.

When we begin to trust our own understanding without reference to the God who loves and made us, it will be as if the ground beneath our feet begins to shift. Before long, our lives will soon become distorted and will no longer be upright. That is why there are such extremes of ungodliness in society. And just as the cost of propping up the leaning tower of Pisa has been massive, so is the personal and societal cost when people ignore God's Word and do their own thing. Trying to correct lives that have gone off course, without God, is a never-ending never-succeeding roundabout of human effort without godly gain.

To trust in the Lord means to depend on Him totally and not on our own seemingly good, but ungodly, ideas. Our Scripture stresses that we should trust Him with ALL of our heart – not just a 'religious bit' which we are happy for him to have, provided we can keep hold of the rest! Some of the Kings of Israel and Judah were less than whole-hearted in their service of the Lord – and as a result their lives and reigns didn't end well.

God's promises to those who do trust Him wholeheartedly, meaning with ALL of their heart, are many and wonderful – including this one, that He will help us walk along straight paths. Or, as I learned it in the Authorised Version, *"He will direct your paths."*

Many is the time when I have sensed God bringing correction into my life so that the path I was walking on would remain straight and many are the times, also, when I have sensed Him directing my paths so that I would know His will for the next stage of my life. I am so grateful to God for His wisdom – it is beyond human understanding.

Prayer: *Help me, Lord, to trust You at all times and to look for Your clear direction in my life. I pray that You will direct my steps so that the paths I walk on will be those You have prepared for me. In Jesus' Name. Amen.*

Personal Notes

Thank You Heavenly Father for showing me that I need to actively contact Barbara M (co-Lead on Explore B Monthly Grp) to apologise for offending her. Thank You for forgiving me after I confessed to You & repented of this sin (heartlessness), in Jesus Name. AMEN!!!

15

Day 2 – 2/2/19

Walking in the Plans and Purposes of God

"Many are the plans in a man's heart, but it is the Lord's purpose that prevails." Proverbs 19:21

God has a plan and a purpose for each one of our lives. We may have lots of ideas about what we would like to do with the years that stretch before us, but our ideas need to be tested and submitted to the great Planner. One of the greatest of the old hymns expresses so powerfully what should be the desire of our heart:

> *Guide me, O Thou great Redeemer;*
> *Pilgrim through this barren land;*
> *I am weak, but Thou art mighty,*
> *Hold me with Thy pow'rful hand.*

16

It doesn't matter whether we still have most of our life to live, or are wondering if the year ahead might be our last, God still has a strategy and a plan for us. However many years there may be in store, we still have a choice as to how we will fill our time.

God has given each of us free will. But if our free will is not gladly surrendered to His purposes for our lives, then we will be in danger of missing out on God's best for us. Then we could be in danger of coming up against the purposes of God which, as our Scripture indicates, will prevail. It's far better to be flowing in the will and purposes of God gladly, than to discover at a later time that you have been going in the opposite direction to God's plan for your life.

God is Creator – and we are made in His image and likeness – that means that we are creative also. He rejoices to inspire our own creativity and to fill our minds with plans which will be a blessing to us personally and which will also be purposeful in respect of the Kingdom of God.

I've found on many occasions that when we walk in fellowship and obedience with Him, God gives us vision and He opens up the way ahead so that the vision He has given becomes the purposes of God for us.

You really matter to God. He loves you unconditionally. He doesn't condemn you because of mistakes in the past but wants to forgive you, heal you from their consequences and equip you for the days ahead. He only wants His best for your life. There are many strands to each one of our lives – when God weaves those strands together He creates a beautiful tapestry.

Sometimes it is a strand which seemed of little consequence at the time, that proves to be of great significance in later years. We cannot avoid having to live in a fallen world that has rejected the God who made it. And we may be going through tough times as a result, but no matter how difficult the journey may be, God has assured us that he will be with us every step of the way.

Prayer: *Thank You, Jesus, for being my Redeemer and for Your commitment to being my Guide through life. Forgive me, Lord, when I have tried to do things that were not Your best for me and help me, Lord, to see how precious it is to be Your representative in working out Your purposes. In Jesus' Name, Amen.*

Personal Notes

Thank You LORD for providing the oppartunity to speak, hopefully in love, to the Director about the tricky situation currently existing in the Team at Ellel Grange.

Day 3 – 3/2/19

Honouring the Lord

"Honour the Lord with your wealth, with the first-fruits of all your crops, then your barns will be filled to overflowing, and your vats will brim over with new wine." (Proverbs 3:9-10)

There are many scientific laws which govern the physical universe in which we live. Gravity, for example, keeps our feet firmly on the ground and makes things feel heavy. If you drop something it will always fall downwards. This is the fundamental law which holds our universe together, keeps planet Earth in place going round the sun, and the moon in place going round the Earth. We all know the importance of respecting these physical laws and are careful not to fall off the edge of a building or a cliff, for we know that if we do we will come to harm.

But, in addition to all the physical laws that scientists have discovered, there are spiritual laws which exist within God's spiritual universe which God has shared with us in His Word. And if we ignore those spiritual laws then there will also be consequences.

Knowledge of God's spiritual laws is intended to be a blessing for us. For, if we choose to do those things that God has told us not to do, such as worship idols or commit adultery, then we are putting ourselves outside of God's protection and that would be dangerous. It would be like trying to defy gravity by stepping off the edge of a cliff!

If we don't do the things that God has told us to do, such as honour our father and our mother, then we will miss out on the many blessings that result, for example, from honouring our parents. Our Scripture for today highlights one of those spiritual laws through which God would want to bless us – honouring the Lord with our wealth.

To honour God means to worship Him. We worship by our love and obedience to Him and, for example, by giving Him of our time, by listening to His voice, by doing those things that please Him, and singing His praises. And one of the spiritual laws that is intrinsic to our relationship with God is that when we honour Him He chooses to bless us. If you read Deuteronomy 28:1-14, you will see some of the many ways God chose to bless His people when they honoured Him with their obedience.

And part of honouring God is to give to Him the first fruits of whatever the Lord leads us to do, to bring to him our tithes and offerings and to give, with a thankful heart, when the Lord prompts us to share what he has given us with others. That is worship. And as we worship by responding to the promptings of the Holy Spirit to give, the Lord chooses to pour back upon us His blessings, in His way and in His time.

We do not give to God so that we will get a reward – that is the selfish deception of what is sometimes called the 'prosperity Gospel'. But when we give to Him because we love Him and want to worship Him, then God has promised that we will know His blessings in our lives and we can trust His Word. For, as Paul expressed it so powerfully, *"My God will meet all your needs according to His glorious riches in Christ Jesus"* (Philippians 4:19)

Prayer: Thank You, Lord, for the amazing promises that are in Your Word. Forgive me, Lord, for the times when I have withheld from You my worship of giving. Help me, I pray, to learn how to honour You with everything You have given me, so that my giving may be a blessing to others and to You. In Jesus' Name. Amen.

Personal Notes

"Set a guard over my mouth LORD, keep watch over the door of my lips." (Psalm 141:3) Especially as I fellowship with one of my housemates today.

Day 4 — 4/2/19

Learning How to Live Longer!

"The fear of the LORD is the beginning of wisdom, and knowledge of the Holy One is understanding. For through me your days will be many, and years will be added to your life." Proverbs 9:10-11

Living longer is the dream of most men and women, but not many in today's world discover one of the most precious keys to a long life, which is found in today's Scripture! And the reason they don't find it is because they are ignorant of what God says in His Word.

Holy fear of a holy God is the first pillar of truth from these verses, which is critical for life. If we learn to live in awe and reverence of the God, who loves us so much, then we are choosing to live in holy fear. That doesn't mean we will be afraid of Him, for there is no reason why we should fear love. But, as a result, we will to want to do what is right and will not want to do those things that grieve Him by our stepping off His pathway for our life.

But the second pillar – knowledge of the Holy One – is equally important. Knowing everything we can discover from God's Word about His nature and character will give us an understanding of God and His ways which will help us fulfil His purposes for our life. This is one of the prime reasons why we need to daily feed our spirits with reading from the Bible, for it is here that we learn about Him.

People who know me, because they have worked with me in Ellel Ministries for many years, have come to understand how I think and what I would do in many different circumstances. As a result, I have complete confidence and trust in them and the way they run the different Ellel Centres around the world. If they didn't know me, they wouldn't understand the heart of the ministry and know what to do in each situation. They would either constantly have to get in touch with me to ask for an opinion, or they would make mistakes, because they would be acting without an understanding of either my heart or the way God has led us to serve Him in the ministry.

In just the same way we need to get to know the heart of God – and once we have His heart and He has ours, we can move forward in faith and trust, confident that He will lead us.

And when we are doing those things that please Him, we can be confident also that we won't be doing those things that could have the effect of shortening our lives. This is easy to understand when you see the medical statistics about the shortened life expectancy of those who are addicted to drugs, or catch sexually transmitted diseases through promiscuous sexual relationships. There is plenty of evidence in the daily news of our nations that living an ungodly life can have a serious life-shortening effect.

Living a holy life in the fear of God is not living a dull life. It is the most challenging and exciting life imaginable. And God promises to add years to our life when we understand and walk in His ways!

Prayer: *Thank You, Lord, for the wonderful promises we find in Your Word. Help me to get to know You better and I ask that Your Holy Spirit will fill me day by day with His power to strengthen me against temptation and be a blessing to You and to others. In Jesus' Name, Amen*

Personal Notes

Thank You LORD for Your help
yesterday through the tough time
of speaking truth in love to my
housemate as best as I knew how
to. May Your Will be done in the
whole situation to the glory of Your
Name, LORD Jesus. AMEN!!!

Day 5 – 5/2/19

Money – Servant or Idol?

"Whoever trusts in his riches will fail, but the righteous will thrive like a green leaf." (Proverbs 11:28)

The book of Proverbs has lots to say about the three most dangerous temptations, money, sex and power. These temptations are a constant threat, even to believers, no matter how far they have run in their personal race of life.

Money is one of life's essentials. Without it we cannot buy the necessities of life such as food, clothing and shelter. With it everything we could ever want or dream of becomes possible. Whenever there is a great natural disaster our television screens are full of appeals – what for? For money. For with money the charitable agencies can supply the needs of suffering people.

Scripture encourages us to consider that everything we

25

have belongs to God – and to be generous with our giving to those in need. But because money can buy anything, wanting more can be a dangerous temptation. For money cannot only buy good things, it can also be used for purposes that will take our eyes off God, lead us astray and consume our soul.

There is nothing that can so quickly grow a spiritual cataract over our eyes as greed for money. It can have the effect of blinding us so that we cannot see the deceptive traps we may be falling into. And then, when we have acquired a lot of money, fear takes hold. For when you have started to put your trust in money, as the means of doing whatever you want, instead of trusting in God as your provider (*Jehovah Jireh*), you are trusting in what has become an idol in your heart. And idolatry is driven by fear rather than love.

The fear of not having enough makes people desperate to protect what they have. And the fear of losing it can turn the rich from being generous givers into the meanest of people, as portrayed by Chares Dickens in his amazing novel *'A Christmas Carol'*. The name of Dickens' character, Ebenezer Scrooge, gave birth to a new word in the English language – a 'scrooge', a mean, miserly and unhappy person, even though rich in this world's goods.

Those who depend on their riches are very short-sighted people. For, as our Scripture tells us, those who *"trust in riches will fail"* and Proverbs 27:24 adds to this by saying, *"riches do not endure forever."* And when the Scriptures talk about not lasting for ever, they are contrasting the perspectives of time and eternity, not just saying that money won't last for ever here on Earth.

We may die rich people, but where is the treasure of our heart located? If it is in the wealth we are leaving behind, we have problems, as Jesus explained in His parable of the rich farmer in Matthew 12:13-21. The man wanted to build bigger barns in which he could store all his grain and all his goods, so that he could then *"take life easy; eat, drink and be merry."*

But God's assessment of this man's objectives was very different. The man had been blinded by his riches to eternal truths and in the story God said to him, *"You fool! This very night your life will be demanded from you. Then, who will get what you have prepared for yourself? This is how it will be with anyone who stores up things for himself but is not rich towards God."*

Money can be a means of huge provision and blessing. But it can also be a self-destructive trap. I pray that you will learn to take your eyes off what you have in time and focus on what you can take with you into eternity. *"For where your treasure is, there your heart will be also"* Matthew 6:21. When we are living righteous lives and our heart's focus is right we will, as our Scripture tells us, thrive – without the need to be trusting in riches, for they will fail.

Prayer: Help me, Lord, to value Your provision and to trust You for all I need. Forgive me, Lord, for the times when I have taken my eyes off You and trusted in my possessions instead of You. Give me Your wisdom to have a right balance in my life, to be generous with what You have given me, and to keep my focus on You – the treasure of my heart. In Jesus' Name. Amen.

Personal Notes

Thank You LORD for the gift
of life, which we sometimes
take for granted. Help us
to focus on You on this
daily journey of life & to
depend on Your Heavenly
glorious riches in Christ
Jesus, now & always.
AMEN !!!

Day 6 – 6/2/19

Satan's Trap

"For a man's ways are in full view of the Lord, and he examines all his paths. The evil deeds of a wicked man ensnare him; the cords of his sin hold him fast." (Proverbs 5:21-22)

The book of Proverbs is full of amazing wisdom to help guide the believer along the road of life and avoid Satan's pitfalls. Almost three whole chapters are devoted to the consequences of sexual sin. This must, therefore, be a very serious issue for God if His warnings against sexual sin and adultery should have such prominence.

Proverbs isn't the only place in the Bible where the warnings are so specific. In his letter to the Galatians (5:19-21) for example, Paul lists sexual immorality amongst the sins that people do which could disinherit them from the Kingdom of God. To the Ephesians he said (5:3) *"among you there must not be even a hint of sexual immorality."* And, of course, Jesus himself said that *"anyone who looks at a woman lustfully has already committed adultery with her in his heart"* (Matthew 5:28). Jesus knew that lust of the eyes precedes the lustful fulfilment of a wrong physical relationship. And Paul reminded believers (in 1 Corinthians 10:12), *"If you think you are standing firm, be careful that you don't fall."*

So, why is sexual sin so dangerous that it merits so many scriptural warnings, in addition to the seventh commandment not to commit adultery? The heart of the answer lies in our Scripture for today which comes at the end of Proverbs Chapter 5, which is headed in my Bible, **Warning Against Adultery**. In 1 Corinthians 6:18 Paul warns believers to *"Flee from sexual immorality. All other sins a man commits are outside his own body, but he who sins sexually sins against his own body."* In these two verses we have an important answer to the question and enormous wisdom which, if followed, can be truly life-saving.

When a man and a woman enter into marriage and, thereby, into a godly sexual relationship, they are entering into a covenantal, God-ordained, union by which the man and the woman become one with and part of each other. A similar, but ungodly, union also takes place when a sexual relationship takes place outside of marriage. But this time, instead of it being a union which is blessed by God, it is sinful bondage.

For, as our Scripture says, the cords of such sin hold a man fast. He is now joined with someone in a union which

God did not intend and which He cannot bless. Not only, therefore, is the sin against God, it is, as Paul said, a sin against your own body. For, you have now joined your body, indeed your whole being, to someone else who, as a result, has spiritual access to and, even, influence over who you are – a privilege that God had reserved for a husband-wife relationship.

Every time a person enters into an ungodly sexual relationship, they lose something of their own identity to that sexual partner, and gain something of the identity of the person they have slept with. No wonder Proverbs describes sexual sin as cords which hold us fast. And in Proverbs 6:32 it says *"A man who commits adultery lacks judgement, whoever does so destroys himself."* The pleasure may be for a moment, but it is like pressing a self-destruct button to our own identity.

Praise God that there is a way out of the mess. In 1 Corinthians 6 Paul lists many of the sexual sins people can commit, but in verse 11 he states the unequivocal good news that, *"That is what some of you were. But you were washed, you were sanctified, you were justified in the name of the Lord Jesus Christ and by the Spirit of our God."* He was simply stating the wonderful Gospel truth that where there is true repentance there can be forgiveness and healing – even from the consequences of sexual sin.

Prayer: *Thank You, Lord, that Your Word warns us of the dangers of sexual sin. I ask You, Lord, to forgive me and cleanse me from every bit of sexual uncleanness in my life. And where there have been wrong relationships, I ask you to break the cords* *of bondage, so that I might be free to serve you, unimpeded by the consequences of my sin. In Jesus' Name, Amen.*

Personal Notes

HALLELUYAH !!!
Amen, Amen, Amen!

7/2/19

Thank LORD for helping me with the teaching yesterday and for using it to bring glory to You in Jesus' Name. AMEN !!!

Day 7 – 7/2/18

Laziness, Work and Wealth!

"Lazy hands make a man poor, but diligent hands bring wealth. He who gathers crops in summer is a wise son, but he who sleeps during harvest is a disgraceful son." Proverbs 10:4-5

I was recently reading about a man who, at the age of sixty, heard that he might have a terminal condition. Instead of bemoaning his misfortune, he resolved to work harder than ever to do those things which mattered most to him before he died! In the following years he wrote many books and achieved a great deal. At the age of 92 he was still writing, having long since seen off his supposed terminal condition! He was definitely not lazy, and he became very wealthy as a result of all the work he did.

There is no doubt that the Scripture for today is true –

hard work and diligence do bring reward and wealth, especially when what you do is under the leadership of God's Holy Spirit, properly applied with wisdom. Laziness is something that is universally condemned throughout the Scriptures. Paul was very blunt in his letter to the Thessalonians when he said, *"If a man will not work, he shall not eat"* (2 Thessalonians 3:10). Through my years in business I learnt the hard way that good ideas, even God ideas, will remain as such if you don't put in the work to make them happen.

There are seasons of harvest in all of our lives, when things have built up to a point of fulfilment – and that is definitely not a season to take time off and rest! For then, if the crop is not reaped, poverty will result. But it is also true, that if the ground is not properly prepared and the seed is not sown, there will not be any harvest at all! So, in every stage of life there is work to do, because in every season there is a purpose to fulfil.

And this is just as true in terms of the spiritual work that we do for the Kingdom of God. I was part of the team that worked behind the scenes to prepare for the last major mission that Billy Graham led in the UK. It was called Mission England. There was a great harvest of people who gave their lives to the Lord at the events, which were the spiritual equivalent of a farmer's harvest crop. But those who worked behind the scenes had been working incredibly hard preparing the ground, for at least three years, making sure that every single detail had been thought through in advance of the time of harvest. Lives were changed and transformed at harvest time because the 'farmers' had been doing their work.

There is no shortage of work we can do for the Kingdom of God – let us do it with all our hearts knowing that the size and the quality of the harvest depends on the bit we do!

Prayer: *Thank You, Lord, for the warnings of Scripture to not be lazy. Forgive me, Lord, for times in my life when I have been deliberately lazy. Help me to be wise at every stage of my life and to learn Your wisdom about the things you want me to do – and then to do them with all my heart. In Jesus' name, Amen.*

Personal Notes

Thank You my Heavenly
Father for this new day
that You have made.
Help us to rejoice & be
glad in it and to do all
that You have assigned for
us to do that You will be
glorified in our lives, in
Jesus' Name. AMEN!!!

Day 8 – 8/2/19

False Accusations

"Do not accuse a man for no reason – when he has done you no harm." Proverbs 3:30

Telling lies in order to accuse a person falsely is a heinous crime. Damaging the reputation of someone is an act of robbery of far greater significance than stealing some of their goods – you are stealing their good name. Goods can be replaced, but when 'mud' has been thrown at someone by telling lies about them for some ulterior motive, the sad fact is that some of that 'mud' will stick in the minds of those who hear. They will think that there must be at least a grain of truth in what is being said, even if there isn't!

Jesus suffered greatly from such false accusations. The words of the Pharisees, who concocted false stories about Him, would eventually be used to drive the nails through His hands and His feet when He was crucified. Yes, ruining someone's reputation by false accusation is a serious sin – it's like an act of murder.

We need to be very careful, therefore, when talking about others disrespectfully. We need to be especially careful about pointing the finger at others when we are trying to cover up secret sin in our own life. Jesus hated and condemned such hypocrisy. At one time I was publicly accused, in the most abusive and degrading sort of way by the minister of a large church, that I was in deception, because I was bringing healing and deliverance to Christians. I couldn't understand why this man, whom I had never met, was so keen to destroy me and my reputation. But a few years later it was discovered that he had had a secret ungodly relationship for many years. His fear of being exposed had driven him to attack any ministry that might, with discernment, see what was happening in his own life!

The Pharisees brought to Jesus a woman who had been caught in an act of adultery (John 8:3-11). They wanted to see if He would be true to the law of Moses and say she should be stoned to death. But in response, Jesus challenged the hearts of her accusers and said something like, *"OK, but only throw a stone if you are without sin!"* Jesus knew what was in their hearts and that they had deliberately brought this woman to Jesus in order to try and trap Him. Their motives were evil.

If you've been falsely accused in a public place, you will know the pain that lying words can cause. There is only one remedy for the pain within – forgiveness and God's inner comfort. Yes, they may not deserve to be forgiven – but Jesus died for our sins and we don't deserve to be forgiven either! To speak out forgiveness of those who have accused us falsely is like cutting the ropes that have tied those false accusations to our heart.

And if we've been guilty of hypocritically speaking negatively about other people, for whatever reason – and especially when the things we are saying could just as easily be said of us – then it's time for personal repentance, asking God for forgiveness and a change of heart.

Prayer: *I am sorry, Lord, for the times when I have said wrong things about other people, for whatever reason. Please forgive me. And help me, Lord, to speak out my forgiveness of those who have hurt me with their false words. In Jesus' Name, Amen.*

Personal Notes

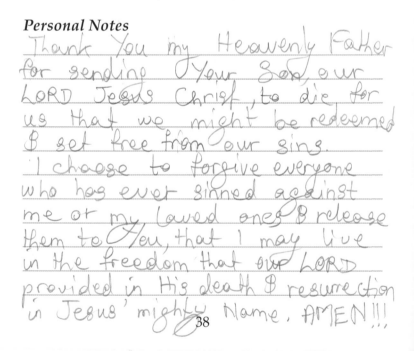

Thank You my Heavenly Father
for sending Your Son, our
LORD Jesus Christ, to die for
us that we might be redeemed
& set free from our sins.
I choose to forgive everyone
who has ever sinned against
me or my loved ones & release
them to You, that I may live
in the freedom that our LORD
provided in His death & resurrection
in Jesus' mighty Name, AMEN!!!

Day 9 – 9/2/18

How wise are you?

"Do not rebuke a mocker or he will hate you; rebuke a wise man and he will love you. Instruct a wise man and he will be wiser still; teach a righteous man and he will add to his learning." Proverbs 9:8-9

It's never easy to receive correction, especially when you believe that you're right! But Proverbs 9 warns us that how we receive correction can be an indicator of how wise we are! For every time that we are corrected is an opportunity to learn and become wiser still.

I soon learnt as a teenager that there were things I had got wrong – and that if I didn't receive the correction gladly, I would be on a very slippery downhill slope and that soon there would be a price to pay! I never liked receiving correction, for it showed up my own ignorance. My pride had been dented!

Without correction, I would never have learned some of life's most important lessons. Students would never grow wiser if their teachers marked their schoolwork as if it was right, when it was wrong. Receiving correction is a vital part of the learning and growing process. And in the school of life we never cease to be students!

But when it comes to correcting others in adult life, we first need to be very discerning of their heart attitude. Today's Scripture reminds us that if the heart of someone is filled with mockery, they will not only refuse to receive correction, but they will actually hate you. And hatred is a murderous weapon which lies at the root of much evil intent. You can't reason with someone who is motivated by hatred and, sadly, they usually have to learn life's lessons the hard way. Wisdom says that sometimes we have to wait until a person is ready to listen before it is possible to bring any correction into their lives.

So, how do you react when you sense the Lord is wanting to confront and correct you? Are you ready to listen? Do you welcome His invitation when He says, as in the words of Isaiah 1:18, *"Come now, let us reason together, says the LORD: though your sins are like scarlet, they shall be as white as snow; though they are red as crimson, they shall be like wool".*

The prophet Nathan had to confront David about his sin of adultery with Bathsheba, and the murder of her husband, Uriah (2 Samuel 12). David had two choices – do I humble myself, own up and repent? Or do I rebel and kill God's prophet? Mercifully, he made the right choice. Nothing could undo what he had done, but the way was now open for God to forgive and restore him. Psalm 51 is David's expression of his confession and repentance.

So how would you have responded if you had been in David's shoes. Would you have resisted the loving entreaties of the Lord when your behaviour was so dramatically challenged? In verses 19 and 20 of chapter 1, Isaiah goes on to say that *"if you are willing and obedient, you will eat the best from the land"* but warns us of serious consequences if we rebel against God's word.

A wise man will listen to the Lord and choose to walk in His ways. Even though David had sinned grievously, he was, nevertheless, a wise man and through this experience learned lessons that he would never forget!

Prayer: *Thank You, Lord, for both the challenge and the encouragement of Your word. Forgive me, Lord, for those times when I have responded badly to necessary correction. Help me to receive Your correction gladly when You see me going off course, so that I will grow wiser and know more of your blessing. In Jesus' Name, Amen.*

Personal Notes

"Set a guard over my mouth, O LORD, keep watch over the door of my lips" Psalm 141:3
May You be glorified in my teaching on Explore today in Jesus' Name. AMEN!

Day 10 – 10/2/19

Pure or Polluted?

"Like a muddied spring or a polluted well is a righteous man who gives way to the wicked." (Proverbs 25:26)

Springs and wells are sources of pure water – water which quenches the thirst, satisfies the taste and is life-giving to all who drink it. But if that life-giving water has become polluted or muddied, then it is undrinkable. It is no longer life-giving, but could even be life-threatening. When a river becomes polluted with, for example, industrial effluent, the fish in the river die. All the water is still there, but it's what's been added to the water that causes the problem.

In just the same way someone may have lived a righteous life and be known as a true believer, but if the stream of truth that comes from their mouth, or is evident in their life, has become polluted with deceptive beliefs, practices or ungodly living, then their life has become poison to those who 'drink' from that stream. They will be influenced by

42

the pollutants and led astray into the same or similar sins. It only takes a small amount of poison in the water to do massive amounts of damage. In just the same way it only takes a small amount of deception in our lives to have the potential for leading many people astray.

A minister came to ask why I thought it was that so many people in the congregation were getting caught in sexual sin, in spite of being in a church where the Word of God was clearly preached. When I asked about the history of his church's leadership, he told me that a previous minister had been found out having an affair with a member of the choir. He had been asked to leave, and the whole affair was covered up by the leaders because they didn't want to bring the church into disrepute. When a leader sins in this way, a spirit is released into the fellowship and given licence to influence his hearers. I wasn't surprised at the outcome. The 'spiritual air' had become polluted and people were breathing in deception.

No wonder Paul was so urgent in teaching his young disciple Timothy. He told him: *"Watch your life and your doctrine closely. Persevere in them, because if you do, you will save both yourself and your hearers"* (1 Timothy 4:16). The implication is that if we allow pollutants to affect our beliefs and our way of life, then the damage could be fatal – to us individually, and to all those who listen to the music of our lives and are tempted to follow our example!

The fact that we may even have years of godly living behind us, does not mean that we are incapable of being led astray. The enemy will work extra hard to pollute the

43

life stream of those who are in a position to influence others. How important it is that we guard our hearts and are very careful about where we put down our feet on the road of life – only going where the Lord is leading and only doing those things that please Him.

Prayer: *Thank You, Lord, for the warnings that You have placed in Your Word. Thank You that You have put them there to help us stay on the right path throughout our days. I pray that You will cleanse me from my sins, Lord, and help me to keep the water of my life free from pollutants, so that it will always be fresh and life-giving to all with whom I relate or influence. In Jesus' name, Amen.*

Personal Notes

Hallelujah to the king of kings !!!
Thank You LORD for seeing me through the Explore teaching yesterday even though I feel that I could have done better, but You remind me that it is not about me at all but all about You & how You want to us this life You have blessed me with to bless others to your glory. We praise Your Holy Name. AMEN!!!

Day 11 – 11/2/19

Setting a True Course

"He holds victory in store for the upright, He is a shield to those whose walk is blameless, for He guards the course of the just and protects the way of his faithful ones." Proverbs 2:7

Some years ago, I devoted a year of my life to writing an on-line daily training school. My heart's desire was to help people know how to walk in the ways of God and be able to set a true course for their lives. If we truly walk on the path that He has laid out for us, then there are many, many promises in the Scripture pointing out the blessings God has in store for His children. This school is now published in book form as *Journey to Freedom* (*Sovereign World* – UK and *Chosen* – USA).

The many blessings that God promises in His Word are an outworking of His covenant love for His children. This one verse alone promises victory (in the battles of life) to those who are upright – that means those who deliberately make godly choices when facing temptation.

Then we are promised a shield of protection if our walk is blameless. What does that mean? I believe it simply means that when our heart's desire is always for God's Kingdom authority to be established in our lives, that the angels of God will rejoice to be there for us – just as they were for Jesus in His wilderness experience being tested by the devil. We will never know till we reach eternity, just how often we have unknowingly experienced God's protection and deliverance.

One day, as I was driving my car, I had to turn to the left up a long gentle hill. As I put my foot down and accelerated away, the driver's door of my car suddenly flung open for no known reason. Immediately I took my foot off the gas, applied the brake, slowed right down and stretched out my hand to close the door. Then, as I looked up again at the road ahead, a young child on a tricycle came hurtling down a sloping driveway from a house and straight out onto the road where I would have been, had the door not mysteriously flung open at that critical moment. I have no doubt that God saved that child's life, and me from the terrible trauma of having killed a child.

When setting sail for a long voyage, the most important thing we need to know is how to navigate. If we cannot set a true course, we will be lost at sea forever. When we set out to be just and fair in all we think, say and do, God promises us His wisdom as we plot the course of our lives.

– not just in the overall big picture of where we are going, but also in the micro-details of today's part of the journey. He is a faithful God. Halleluyah!!!

What tremendous blessings come from our walking in the ways of the Lord. Psalm 19:7 expresses the blessings in terms of revival! All over the world many of God's people are crying out to Him for revival. But God's Word tells us that we can have personal revival wherever we are – all that God looks for is the heart that is turned towards Him and a will that has chosen to respond in obedience to His love!

Prayer: *Thank You, Lord, for the many times Your hand of protection and direction has been operating in my life. Help me to always have such a heart after You and Your ways, that I will consistently choose to follow You in all the activities and details of my life, knowing that You will guide and direct my steps. In Jesus' Name, Amen.*

Personal Notes

Heavenly Father, I pray that You go ahead of me to the GP appointment this morning to prepare the way for the healing of the pain & twinges in my lower back in Jesus' Name to Your Glory. AMEN!!! Oh please heal Minnette's back too... AMEN!!!

Day 12 – 12/2/19

Resist Enticement

"My son, if sinners entice you, do not give in to them . . . do not go along with them, do not set foot on their paths; for their feet rush into sin." Proverbs 1: 10,15-16

The word 'entice' means to tempt, or to lead astray. It carries with it all the connotations of exciting, but ungodly, activities – things which fascinate the carnal nature and which, if we are honest, all of us can be vulnerable to from time to time. Everything from greed to lust, and a whole lot of desires between these two extremes, can get stirred up when enticement is in the air!

In these very testing days, when many people are struggling to hold things together financially and moral boundaries are disintegrating like snow in the sun, many are having to fight a sense of hopelessness, even despair. At times like this, enticement is especially dangerous. People look for some form of 'comfort' or 'escape' from the pressures they are enduring and are that much more vulnerable to temptations when they come – whether that temptation comes in the form of making money, having a wrong relationship or simply indulging in selfish and unproductive activity.

When times are tough, whether that season is totally personal to you or part of a national or international situation, the enemy will always try to take advantage of what's going on, to entice you into something ungodly. He tries to stand in the place of God and be a source of comfort, not telling his victims that his sort of comfort will always prove to be false.

Paul was very explicit about the only source of true comfort when he said, *"Praise be to the God and Father of our Lord Jesus Christ, the Father of compassion and the God of all comfort, who comforts us in all our troubles, so that we can comfort those in any trouble with the comfort we ourselves have received from God"* (2 Corinthians 1:3,4).

Herein lies a model for each one of our lives. Once we have learned how to receive true relational comfort from Father God for ourselves, without seeking the enticements of the enemy, we are then equipped to be able to give the same unconditional loving comfort to others, who may not yet have learned how to draw on the Father's love for their own inner comfort. In so doing we become the hands and heart of God to them and a means of preventing people from seeking the enticements of the enemy and being led astray because of their unmet need.

When John penned the letters from Jesus to the seven Churches, recorded in Revelation 2 and 3, each one highlighted issues and problems that needed to be dealt with in the churches, but then ended with strong words of encouragement to endure and overcome. Jesus knew that, in testing times, the enemy would want to rob them of their inheritance.

So, I urge you not to let anyone be used by the enemy to entice you to sample the pleasures of what John Bunyan called *Vanity Fair,* in his amazing book, *Pilgrim's Progress. Vanity Fair* displays all the enticements of the enemy and is designed by Satan to rob you of your inheritance in God. Each of us must learn to ignore all such enticements and press on, win through and keep running the race of life till that day when the gates of Heaven open at the end of the journey!

Prayer: *I am sorry, Lord, for those times when I have sought false comfort through the enemy's enticements. Help me, Lord, to recognise enticements of the enemy when they come and then to endure and overcome whatever obstacles stand in the way of my destiny in God. In Jesus' Name, Amen.*

Personal Notes

I Praise You Heavenly Father for Your Mercies which are new every marning, in Jesus' Name. AMEN!!! Great is Your Faithfulness O LORD!!!

Day 13 – 13/2/19

Honesty IS the Best Policy

"Kings detest wrongdoing, for a throne is established through righteousness. Kings take pleasure in honest lips, they value a man who speaks the truth." Proverbs 16:12-13

Some time ago there were the most extraordinary scenes in the British Houses of Parliament. Members of Parliament (MPs) were suddenly rushing to pay back money to the Government that they should never have taken!

All MPs are rightfully entitled to claim for necessary expenses in doing their job, but for years there had been a culture of dishonesty in the seat of government. Many MPs, of all political parties, were caught red-handed claiming money by way of expenses, which had nothing whatsoever to do with the job they were doing. And the nation was rightfully outraged.

These people, who were responsible for putting laws into place, which other people have to obey, had been systematically and dishonestly milking the system for their own benefit. But when they were all exposed (by an investigative journalist on a national newspaper), they were all desperately trying to pay the money back, thinking that if they paid it back quickly, they could get away with keeping their reputation. Never before had I seen such a display of public hypocrisy!

I fear for any nation when there is unrighteousness at its core. For, as our scripture for today says, thrones (governments) are established through righteousness. The converse of this is that governments are destroyed by unrighteousness.

The stories of the Kings of Israel and Judah contain many illustrations of what can happen when governments get it wrong. Read how Jehoshaphat, for example, wrongfully entered into a business relationship to build a fleet of ships with the evil King Amaziah (2 Chronicles 20:35-37). He lost God's protection and the whole of the fleet was destroyed!

But before we come down with a heavy hand of judgement upon those in public office who have certainly acted without integrity (not all MPs were implicated, many had acted with total honesty and not claimed any money falsely), let us examine our own hearts.

Is it not possible that there could be things in our own

lives (things we think about, say or do) that are dishonest and, therefore, ungodly? And I wonder how we would be behaving now if an angelic journalist on a 'Kingdom Newspaper' were to publicly expose these things for everyone else to know about? My guess is that we might be moving very quickly to try and put things right!

One day, at the end of time, everything that's unconfessed and unforgiven will be exposed for all to see. So, perhaps we should learn from this sad episode in British parliamentary history and seek to put things right in our own lives now, and not wait for the public exposure that would otherwise come to all in eternity. In that way our lives, our families, our churches, our cities and even our nations can be established in righteousness – and be strong.

Prayer: Lord, I am sorry for the deceptions operating in both my nation and my own private life. I ask that You will forgive me for all the dishonest hidden things that have operated in my life, and help me to put things right now. Thank You that Your Word clearly shows us what is right and what is wrong. In Jesus' Name, Amen.

Personal Notes

Thank You Heavenly Father for this new day that You have made, help us all to rejoice & be glad in it, in Jesus Name, AMEN!!!

Day 14 – 14/2/19

An Undefendable City

"Like a city whose walls are broken down is a man who lacks self-control." Proverbs 25:28

A while ago my wife and I visited Hadrian's Wall – that huge stone wall which crosses from the west to the east of northern England. It was built by the Romans to protect this furthermost border of the Roman Empire from the wild and dangerous Scots, who lived in the hill country beyond the wall! As I looked at this amazing structure, much of which still stands strong and wide today, after nearly two thousand years, I imagined how difficult it would be for invaders to cross the wall in the face of the constant patrols of Roman soldiers, who paraded up and down the top of the wall, twenty-four hours a day.

There are many ancient cities in the world also, which are surrounded by high strong walls as a defence against invading armies. It was news of the broken-down walls of Jerusalem (Nehemiah 1:3) which moved Nehemiah's heart, as he prayed for his home city and his people. The news that the walls were still broken down and the gates burnt brought him to grief. He knew God was calling him to do something about it. Nehemiah's book covers the whole story from beginning to end, of how God used him to take on and complete the task and restore the safety of the city. Without complete walls, the city was defenceless.

Today's Scripture likens the broken-down walls of a city to the broken-down walls of a person's life. Control of our conduct and behaviour is a vital protection against the invasion of the enemy into our lives. Paul explained very carefully in Galatians 6:7-8 how there are consequences for not living a life which is self-controlled and in godly order. The fact is, just as a city with broken-down walls is undefendable – a person's life which is out of control, is also undefendable.

Without the Holy Spirit, none of us will have the strength to resist the attacks of the enemy. We all need that spirit of self-control that the Lord will give us if we ask Him. The problem is that many people enjoy too much the things that come in through the gap in our defences, and the Lord can't help us win a battle which we actually want to lose!

A lady asked for prayer. There were issues in her life that seemed impossible for her to overcome. But during the teaching she had been convicted about an area in her life where her personal walls were well and truly broken down. As the office manager of the company where she worked, she was responsible for handling all the petty cash of the company. In her heart she believed she was worth more to the company than she actually got paid. So, for many years she had systematically fiddled the books and paid herself extra out of petty cash.

The teaching from God's words brought conviction into her heart. She realised that over the years she had stolen many thousands of dollars from the people who trusted her to handle the petty cash with integrity. It was not surprising, therefore, that God couldn't answer her prayers while there was such a glaring hole in the walls of her life. The key to her healing came when, in tears of deep repentance, she started to put matters right – both with God and her employers.

There are many possible reasons why the walls of our personal city could be broken down due to lack of self-control. Let's pray that God will give each of us the desire for all the gaps in our defences to be filled in and then ask Him to show us how to do it. Then our lives will be strong and effective for Him – and what's more, we will be more blessed than we ever dreamed possible!

Prayer: *Help me, Lord, to identify those areas of my life where there are gaps in the defences of my soul. I choose now to want to have defendable walls, so that the enemy will no longer have access to the centre of my life. In Jesus' Name, Amen.*

Personal Notes

Thank You my Heavenly Father
for this new day that You
have made. Help us to rejoice
& be glad in it!
Watch over all my loved ones
- Seny, Ismail/Sarah & baby
Opeolu, Ferida (especially as
she travels in Malaysia in the
next 2 weeks) and Rashid
(as he takes care of our home while
Ferida is away).
Cover us all in the blood of
Jesus & cover all our homes,
places of work & watch over
our coming & going both now
& forever more in Jesus Name.
AMEN.!!!

Day 15 — 15/2/19

The Highway Code for God-Blessed Living

"Where there is no revelation, the people cast off restraint; but blessed is he who keeps the law." Proverbs 29:18

The Highway Code is a document which sets out in detail and with great clarity exactly what drivers in the UK can and cannot do on British roads. It is an important publication which is at the heart of all road safety. If people do not know or understand the Highway Code, then they will, inevitably, make mistakes. When drivers ignore these wise legal restraints, accidents, injuries and, even, death could be the result.

Without wise restraints there is always danger. This is true in many areas of life. When there was much heavy rain in the UK, some areas of the country were subject to severe flooding. People even died when the flood waters broke the banks of a river and the formerly placid stream became a raging torrent, sweeping away everything in its path.

A river is a wonderful blessing when it is contained within the restraint of its banks, but once the restraint has been breached the water goes everywhere, people's homes are flooded and there is danger. Strong restraints make the river safe.

The laws of God are meant to act like the Highway Code and the banks of a river, restraining our behaviour so that we never venture into dangerous territory. But when people lose an appreciation of the fact that God's laws are designed by Him to keep us safe, then it's easy to succumb to the temptations which would take us beyond those barriers of safety.

As I wrote this devotional, the newspapers were full of news of the tragic death of one of Britain's richest women – she had everything she could possibly have wanted. Her house was said to have been worth seventy million pounds. But she and her husband had lived a life without restraint, addicted to drugs. Her life ended at a tragically early age. If only she had learned to live her life according to the revelation of truth that there is in the Word of God.

When we choose to respect that God's Word truly is a revelation from God Himself and begin to respect the restraints that God in His love and wisdom provided for us, we lay down a foundation of blessing – not only for our own lives, but also for the lives of our children and grandchildren. When we gladly live within those restraints we find ourselves constantly discovering the many blessings God wants us to enjoy as His children.

Because we have free will, however, people find it tempting to laugh at those restraints and choose to live life in their own way. But they will eventually discover that there is a law of sowing and reaping – and it's only good seed that produces a good crop. If you need convincing about the blessings that come to those who keep God's laws, then spend a quiet hour reading Psalm 119. Just as the Highway Code is the blue-print for safe driving, Psalm 119 is the Highway Code for God-blessed living!

Prayer: Thank You, Lord, that You loved us enough to show us how restraints can be a source of blessing in our lives. Help me, Lord, to welcome the application of Your laws in my life. In Jesus's Name, Amen.

Personal Notes

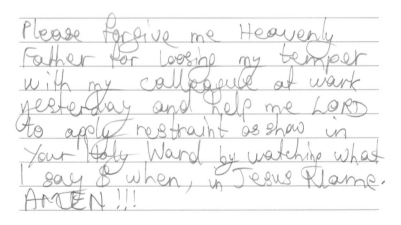

Please forgive me Heavenly
Father for loosing my temper
with my colleague at work
yesterday and help me LORD
to apply restraint as show in
Your Holy Word by watching what
I say & when, in Jesus Klame.
AMEN !!!

Day 16 – 16/2/19

The Lamp of God

"The lamp of the Lord searches the spirit of a man, it searches out his innermost being." Proverbs 20:27

Our eyesight can change over the years and I needed a new pair of glasses. In one part of the test, the optician used a brilliant pin-point of light to look through the lens of my eye and examine the condition of my retina. Her lamp was searching out the innermost recesses of my eyes. I was relieved when she reported that everything was in good order.

In a similar way, the Holy Spirit is the 'lamp of God' and reaches beyond the exterior of our lives to test our spirit and search out the recesses of our innermost being – those places where we can even try and hide things from ourselves. The places where the thoughts and the intentions of our heart can reside and act as motivators of the soul.

61

As a consequence of his extraordinary and life-changing encounter with the Almighty God, the young Isaiah was forced to look at himself afresh. In the face of the blinding light of revelation that came into him as a result of seeing the glory of God, he became acutely aware of his own inner uncleanness. He was totally undone by the experience (Isaiah 6:1-5). Hebrews 4:13 tells us that *"nothing is hidden from God's sight"*. The thoughts and the intentions of our heart are open to His view.

Our innermost being is the source of the decisions we make and the things we do – both good and bad. It is here that the motives of the heart have their origin and Proverbs 16:2 tells us that it is the *"motives that are weighed by the Lord."*

It is so easy for us to deceive ourselves and for our ways to seem innocent to us (as it also says in Proverbs 16:2), even though they may be far from innocent! As a result, we become blinded, even to what those innermost motives are! We need help – and help is at hand. For this Scripture tells us that the lamp of the Lord will search out our innermost being. But we need to give Him permission to show us the truth about ourselves.

So often we pray with people who need help with a seemingly obvious problem, but it isn't the real issue. A Pastor told me I had saved the life of one of his church members. She weighed 350 pounds and was eating herself to death. No amount of self-discipline or prayer seemed to help. As we talked and asked the Lord to shine His lamp on her life, she was reminded of the day when her husband left her by sticking a note on her fridge door to say that he had left her for someone else. On that day she had opened the fridge door and began to comfort herself with what was inside. Twenty years later she was still doing it. When God opened her heart to forgive and receive God's healing, her desire to comfort herself with food disappeared and she lost weight rapidly. Her life was indeed saved through the penetrating light of the Holy Spirit – the lamp of God.

So, our prayer today is simply to ask the Lord to shine His lamp into the recesses of our heart and to show us what He sees! We then need to take time to listen to the Lord and to welcome His presence. It is at times like this that the Lord has not only shown me things that I need to address in my life, but when He has whispered things into my heart that have subsequently become of great significance in the direction my life should take.

Prayer: *Thank You, Lord, that You are able to see into the inner recesses of my heart. Please shine Your lamp and help me to see those things that are displeasing to You, so that, with Your help, I can make lasting and fruitful changes in my life. And then envision me afresh so that the motives of my heart will always be to please You. In Jesus' Name. Amen.*

Personal Notes

O LORD, please shine Your light into my innermost part to show why I get irritated so easily by others, so that I can repent of this sin & let You cleanse me of all unrighteousness, that Your Grace might flow through me to others, in Jesus Name. AMEN!!!

Day 17 – 17/2/19

Rich or Poor?

"Keep falsehood and lies far from me; give me neither poverty nor riches, but give me only my daily bread. Otherwise, I may have too much and disown you and say 'Who is the Lord?' Or I may become poor and steal, and so dishonour the name of my God." Proverbs 30:8-9

We all like having money to spend, but it takes an unusual degree of spiritual wisdom to pray this prayer – a prayer which is designed to help us maintain godly stability in our lives, with an adequate level of income for the life God has called us to live, but not too much!

This Scripture highlights the dangers that can lie at the opposite ends of the scale. If we have too little we may, in desperation, be tempted to use ungodly ways such as dishonesty, cheating or stealing to try and fix things for ourselves. But if we have too much, then the riches we have could take the focus of our eyes off the pathways of life, which the Lord would want us to follow. It's possible to remain faithful to God, even in the extremes of poverty or with the privilege of having wealth, but both extremes are potentially dangerous.

Benjamin Franklin once commented on this dilemma by saying that, *"Contentment makes poor men rich, and discontent makes rich men poor."* He was taking his cue from Paul's words to his trainee evangelist, Timothy: *"But godliness with contentment is great gain. For we brought nothing into the world, and we can take nothing out of it. But if we have food and clothing, we will be content with that. Those who want to get rich fall into temptation and a trap and into many foolish and harmful desires that plunge people into ruin and destruction. For the love of money is a root of all kinds of evil. Some people, eager for money, have wandered from the faith and pierced themselves with many griefs"* (1 Timothy 6:6-11).

Paul's early life had been immersed, as a Pharisee, in the study of the Scriptures and today's verse will have been very familiar to him. No doubt, he had seen the reality of both ends of the spectrum – how poverty and hunger can become an ungodly driving force in a person's life, and how wealth, and the discontent with what one already has, creates the desire for more and more wealth. That also becomes an insatiable driving force.

And when a person has great wealth, the fact that they can buy whatever they want with their money makes their riches an idol which is worshipped every single day. When

God answered Solomon's prayer for wisdom, as a young man, God gave him the ability to know and to speak out God's truth. But in the fleshly areas of his life he ceased to listen to the Holy Spirit's voice of wisdom and finished up being led astray by the women in his life and building temples for them to their pagan gods.

If only Solomon had listened to his own teaching, it would have saved him from many things. Many times people have made *"If only . . ."* comments to me – especially relating to how they had spent their life. They had not learnt to be content with living a godly life and then, twenty or thirty years and more later, they were forced by circumstances to review the consequences of the choices they had made.

Perhaps it's time in your life to learn to be content with God whatever your physical circumstances. To trust Him to be our provider when we are in need and to ask Him for wisdom and courage as to how to use the wealth that we have.

Prayer: *Thank You, Lord, for Your faithfulness. Forgive me, Lord, for times when, out of need, I have been tempted to do wrong things. And for times when my desire for more wealth has unleashed a spirit of greed which has driven me away from You. Help me, Lord, to be content in You – knowing that godly contentment is treasure beyond understanding. In Jesus' Name, Amen.*

Personal Notes

Thank You Heavenly Father
for Your mercies which are
new every morning & for
Your Great Faithfulness
in my life & in the lives of
my family & all our loved
ones, in Jesus' Name. AMEN!!!
I praise Your Holy Name.
Teach me LORD to be
content with what You give
me in this life & with where
You place me, to the glory
of Your Name O LORD.
AMEN!!!

Day 18 – 18/2/19

When I was a Boy

"When I was a boy in my father's house, still tender and an only child of my mother, he taught me and said, "lay hold of my words with all your heart; keep my commands and you will live. Get wisdom, get understanding; do not forget my words or swerve from them." Proverbs 4:3-4

How I thank God that at the age of nine I knelt at my bedside with my father and invited Jesus into my heart. I have never forgotten that most important moment in the whole of my life. I will never cease to be thankful for a Dad (and a Mum) who saw it as their loving duty to teach me the ways of the Lord when I was young – before I reached the impressionable teenage years when it is so easy for young people to go astray and, as they say, *'do their own thing'.*

'Doing their own thing' can be extremely risky, for having the developing physique and unbridled will of a young person, without the maturity of an adult, can lead to people making big mistakes of life-long consequence.

When we learn to respect our elders, we will listen to what they have to say. And the wisdom that comes from their maturity, becomes the wisdom that will help young people negotiate the traps that the enemy never ceases to lay in their paths. We live, however, in a generation in which respect for the wisdom of our elders has been replaced by information acquired at the click of a mouse or via a mobile phone. And information, without the maturity and wisdom as to how it should be used, will always be a massive trap for young people.

Such knowledge will never trump the spiritual wisdom the writer of these Proverbs is referring to. For this is the wisdom from the heart of God which God intended to be passed on from generation to generation.

As I thought about this, I was overwhelmed with a sense of responsibility that parents, grand-parents, great grand-parents, uncles and aunts have to pray for the children in the family and to gently lead them to faith in Jesus when they are young. Then, imparting the wisdom of their years to the upcoming generations, gives them a chance to negotiate the pitfalls of life. With the wisdom of the older generations to aid them on their journey through life, they will be much better equipped to enter into their destiny in God and who knows what blessing there will be down the years as a result?!

Even when we have not personally had the blessing of a human father who taught us God's wisdom when we were young, our heavenly Father has ensured that we can still benefit from the blessing of His wisdom leading and directing our lives, through the written word of God. The world may not respect the precious truths the Bible contains, but we don't have to follow the ways of the world. God has given us freewill and when we use it to make godly choices and not swerve off the Royal Highway laid out for us by the King of Kings, then we can be sure that the promises of God will be as true for us as if we had been taught them from an early age.

Our Scripture for today is a great encouragement to all parents to spend time with their children and let them learn the precious truths in God's Word by hearing them from our lips and seeing our lives being lived in harmony with the commands of God.

Prayer: *Thank You, Lord, for all those who have imparted the wisdom of God into my life. Help me to exercise my own spiritual responsibility by imparting Your Wisdom to the children and young people who are part of my wider family. In Jesus' Name, Amen.*

Personal Notes

Thank You Heavenly Father
for this new day and I put
on my LORD Jesus Christ
as my covering & the covering
for my family now & always,
AMEN!!!

70

Day 19 – 19/2/19

The Currency of Heaven

"Wealth is worthless in the day of wrath, but righteousness delivers from death. The righteousness of the blameless makes a straight way for them, but the wicked are brought down by their own wickedness."
Proverbs 11:4-5

Wealth and riches can be used to bring enormous blessing to many people, if they are used wisely and generously in the Lord's service. We may spend all our lives trying to accumulate large amounts of money – but the fact is, we can only use our physical resources while we are here on earth! Nothing of what we physically own on our earthly pilgrimage will carry any weight or give us any influence when we finally have to face God. We cannot take any of it with us. All our money and human resources will count for nothing on the day which Solomon described here as being 'the day of wrath'.

The power and influence that wealth can exercise on earth is reduced to nothing when we stand before God. Earthly gold, silver and treasure is not the currency of heaven. The currency of heaven is the 'righteousness of the blameless'. Jesus told a parable to help people understand how important it is to be ready, having a good supply of the sort of currency that does carry weight in eternity.

In the parable (see Matthew 25), there were ten girls waiting for the Bridegroom to come. Five had a good supply of oil for their lamps, the others had none. When it became clear that the Bridegroom was coming, panic set in among the five without oil with which to light their lamps, so they went off to try and find some – but it was too late. The Bridegroom came, and they missed their opportunity. Only those who already had oil in their lamps could go with Him.

Jesus is, of course, the Bridegroom and the Body of Christ is the Bride. Only those who have truly humbled themselves at the foot of the cross and received Jesus as their Saviour and Lord are capable of being made righteous and are able to be part of the Bride. And when the fruit of our lives is assessed it is only that which has been done in obedient response to His love that will carry weight when the books are finally opened at the end of time (Revelation 20:11-12).

This is the currency of Heaven, the righteousness that *"delivers from death"* and which makes a way straight ahead of us in the journey of life. It is so vitally important that our trust for daily living is not in whatever resources we may, or may not, have, but in the God who loved us so much that He sent that which was most precious to Him, His Son, to express His love towards us.

When we trust in Him and follow Him in joyful obedience we are storing up for ourselves eternal wealth which can only be measured in the currency of Heaven. While God can use money to facilitate His Kingdom purposes here on Earth, let's not fall into the trap of trusting in what we have on Earth, thinking that this will give us credibility in Heaven. It won't!

Prayer: *Thank You, Lord, for the blessings I can bestow on others, through using whatever resources You have given me, to play my share in building the Kingdom of God. I ask that You will forgive me, Lord, for ever thinking that any earthly wealth I may have accumulated on earth will give me status before You. Help me to be wise with the resources You have given me and to keep my eyes focused on accumulating the currency of Heaven – not the riches of Earth! In Jesus' Name, Amen.*

Personal Notes

Day 20 – 20/2/19

Deaf Ears!

"If anyone turns a deaf ear to the law, even his prayers are detestable. He who leads the upright along an evil path, will fall into his own trap, but the blameless will receive a good inheritance." Proverbs 28:9-10

When someone is said to turn a deaf ear to something, it doesn't mean that they are deaf and can't hear! It simply means they are choosing to ignore what's being said. God's Word very clearly expresses both God's heart of love for mankind and, in His law, He shows us how He wants us to live. The ten commandments are referred to in Deuteronomy 4:13 as God's covenant. God's covenant is an expression of His loving provision for His people. There can be no confusion over what His Word says – especially in the fundamental areas of morality.

But when faced with temptation people have to make

choices in many areas of their lives. They know that choosing to walk in God's ways is the way to enjoy His blessings for, as the second part of our Scripture says, *"the blameless will receive a good inheritance"*. Most believers also know that sin has its consequences as well. But few people realise that in addition to the direct consequences of sin, which is rebellion against God, there is a serious secondary consequence of deliberately turning a deaf ear to what God says in His Word – our prayers are no longer acceptable to God.

This truth was also spoken out by the prophet Isaiah, at a time when God's people were in serious rebellion against Him. *"When you spread out your hands in prayer, I will hide my eyes from you; even if you offer many prayers, I will not listen"* (Isaiah 1:15). So, when we turn a deaf ear towards God's Word and deliberately choose to flaunt His laws, then God responds in like manner – He no longer listens to our prayers. This is a principle that applies to individuals, organisations, congregations and, even, nations, as the people of Israel found out to their cost on numerous occasions.

Often people ask, "Why doesn't God answer my prayers?" While there may be many different answers to this question, the one answer we don't want to hear could be that God is turning a deaf ear towards us because of our deliberate sin! When our behaviour tells God that we don't really care about Him, then it is not surprising that our prayers become an offence to Him. It's not that God doesn't love us and is not interested in our prayers, it's simply that our actions towards Him are speaking louder than the words we might say to Him.

If we want to regain a place of authority in prayer, so that we will know about and experience the power of prayer at work in our lives, then let's determine that the actions of our lives and the words of our lips are truly in harmony with each other. When they are, God has no problem in hearing and answering our prayers! But when our actions are speaking a different language from our lips, then we are in great danger.

Prayer: *Thank You, Lord, for showing me that there can be a relationship between what I do and whether or not You hear and answer my prayers. Forgive me, Lord, for the times when I have deliberately chosen to sin at the same time as thinking You should be answering my prayers. Help me, Lord, to live my whole life in harmony with Your Word so that I can be a person of spiritual integrity and know the blessing of answered prayer. In Jesus' Name, Amen.*

Personal Notes – 21/2/19

Thank You Heavenly Father
for helping me yesterday
in correcting my colleague
in Love without criticism
(hopefully), in Jesus' Name.
AMEN!!

Day 21 - 21/2/19

A Matter of Life and Death

"Whoever gives heed to instruction prospers, and blessed is he who trusts in the Lord . . . there is a way that seems right to a man, but in the end it leads to death." Proverbs 16:20 and 25

It is not wrong to want to prosper – there are many verses in the Bible, which promise prosperity – but the general understanding of what the word 'prosperity' means is significantly different from what the Bible teaches!

As is clear from this verse, one of the keys to becoming prosperous in God's way is not only to listen to the instruction which comes right to our spirit from Him and the Word of God, but to take heed to what the instruction is saying. This means apply the teaching in your life and keep walking forward in obedience.

In the years before the work of Ellel MInistries started I was a publisher, running my own companies. I desperately wanted them to be successful. One day a book proposal came to me in the post through which I thought I could make a lot of money – and become prosperous. The only problem was that God spoke to me in my heart and told me not to have anything to do with the man who was writing that book!

Because I wanted to be prosperous in my own way, I deliberately closed my heart to the instruction of the Lord, thinking that I knew better than God! That was the biggest mistake I ever made in my business career. It very nearly cost me everything I had and at one stage I was hovering between bankruptcy and being murdered.

I was deeply repentant for what I had done and cried out to God for Him to save and deliver me, for the man was threatening to take my very life. God heard my prayer and amazingly delivered me. But I very nearly discovered the hard way the most severe meaning of the second part of this verse, which says, *"there is a way that seems right to a man, but in the end it leads to death."*

Through that experience, I learnt the most important lesson of my life – that God's instructions matter, and that when He speaks it's not a good idea to disobey His voice. On other occasions, when I did obey the Lord and allowed Him to direct my steps and the way I ran the business, I had some remarkable and very blessed business experiences, which led to a very prosperous outcome.

And so, the message I want to emphasise from this Scripture is simply to encourage you to trust God and His Word and to listen for His instruction every day. It could be a matter of life and death! God has promised to show you the way to go, so that you can enjoy the blessing of God's presence with you as you choose to resist the temptations of the evil one and walk in God's ways.

Prayer: *Thank You, Lord, that You have given us vital keys in Your Word to help us live for You and to enjoy the sort of prosperity You have planned for us. Forgive me, Lord, for the times when I've chosen to ignore Your gentle voice of instruction and help me to always have the courage to obey You and Your Word. In the name of Jesus, Amen.*

Personal Notes — 22/2/19

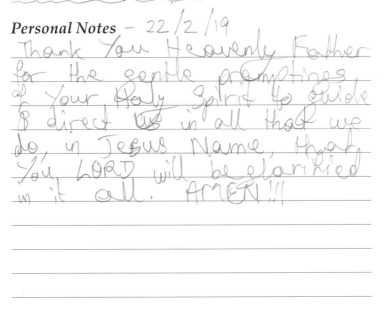

Thank You Heavenly Father
for the gentle promptings
of Your Holy Spirit to guide
& direct us in all that we
do, in Jesus Name, that
You LORD will be glorified
in it all. AMEN !!!

Day 22 — 22/2/19

God's Way of Wisdom

"A fool finds no pleasure in understanding but delights in airing his own opinions . . . he who gets wisdom loves his own soul; he who cherishes understanding prospers." Proverbs 18:2 and 19:8

No-one likes being called a fool – but, sadly, many people behave in a very foolish way in respect of understanding the things of God! Pride and arrogance reign in their life – they think they know best and can do without any input from the God whom modern science has consigned to the dustbin of religious history, as an unnecessary myth! For them, the world invented itself and man is master of their universe.

But not having a knowledge or understanding of God's Word puts them in the situation of being ignorant about the most important things of life! The Psalmist told us that someone who says that there is no God is a fool (Psalm 14:1). So, according to God' Word, a man who is, even, the cleverest scientist on the planet, but who denies the reality of God as Creator, is, simply, a fool.

There are people, however, who don't deny the existence of God, but they are still foolish. They are so full of their own ideas and opinions, that they never stop to think about whether or not they are right or wrong or listen to what others are saying. As our Scripture makes so very clear, they do not even seek to gain understanding. When God was speaking to his people through the prophet Hosea, He said, *"My people are destroyed through lack of knowledge"* (Hosea 4:6).

Faith is, of course, absolutely essential for salvation – for without faith it's impossible to please God (Hebrews 11:6). But when it comes to our day-to-day living, as believers in God, we should always be diligent to gain understanding – about God, the ways of God and the plans of God for us. With both faith and understanding, we will have a better perception on situations as they develop and be in a much better place to make good choices and godly decisions.

Many of the people whom I have had the privilege of ministering to over the years, have had plenty of faith in God, but at times in their lives they made unwise decisions, without seeking God's understanding and wisdom. And those choices sometimes left them with very expensive lifetime consequences.

But the end of our Scripture for today encourages us with

a wonderful promise – that if we cherish understanding and then make godly choices, we will enjoy God's blessing on our lives. This is God's promise to His people.

The word cherish means really love and care for something or someone, treasure, value highly and hold dear within your heart. If we feel like that towards having knowledge and understanding about the things of God, then it will be for us as if the heart of God becomes ours. We will then understand things from His point of view. And there cannot be a better perspective for us to have on life!

Prayer: Help me, Lord, to always seek to gain knowledge and understanding of You and Your ways, so that I will be in a much better position to make godly choices in all the future decisions of my life. In Jesus' Name, Amen.

Personal Notes

> OLUWAKEMI = God Treasures me
>> " Cherishes "
>> " highly values "
>> " really loves "
>> " cares for "
> God holds me dear
>> within His Heart

Day 23 — 23/2/19

Unwelcome Messages!

"He who listens to a life-giving rebuke will be at home among the wise. He who ignores discipline despises himself, but whoever heeds correction gains understanding. The fear of the Lord teaches a man wisdom, and humility comes before honour." Proverbs 15:31-33

There are times in all our lives when we need to hear the truth about ourselves. But, frankly, none of us likes it. The natural instinct of our carnal nature is to rise up to attack the messenger instead of to listen carefully to the message, asking the Lord if there is any truth in what is being said. I can remember several times as a youth rising up on the inside and thinking my father was so wrong in what he was saying. In later life, however, I realised just how right he was at the time and how important his loving correction had been. It saved me from making much more serious mistakes.

In the history of God's people there were many occasions when the prophets brought unwelcome messages. Instead of listening to what God was saying to the people through God's prophetic mouthpiece, they often turned on the prophets who had had the courage to tell the people the truth.

For example, in Isaiah's day the people turned on him saying, *"Don't give us any more visions of what is right, tell us pleasant things, prophesy illusions"* (Isaiah 30:10). This is an extraordinary verse of Scripture. The people knew Isaiah to be a godly man who listened to the heart of God and always spoke the truth. But when the people didn't like hearing what he had to say, instead, they asked this godly man to tell them lies! They did not want to hear the voice of God through Isaiah's corrective words. In pride and arrogance, they wanted to live life in their own ungodly way. When someone speaks correction into our lives, let's be careful not to hastily reject the message.

Today's Scripture contains a salutary warning about the dangers of ignoring the voice of correction. It also gives us a very interesting slant on the consequences of ignoring discipline. It says that he who ignores discipline despises himself! Discipline may not always be given in the best possible way and it's rarely a comfortable experience! But when it comes, we need to weigh it carefully, for if we reject the message and choose to 'shoot' the messenger instead, we are actually despising ourselves.

If you despise someone, you look down on them and don't give them any respect. And if you despise yourself that is exactly what you are doing. You are looking down on yourself and disrespecting the need there may be in your life to prayerfully consider the message and choose to change. The consequences could be serious, as they so often were for God's people when they rejected the messages of God's prophets.

Our Scripture encourages us to listen carefully to the voice of correction, for it is through this that we can gain important understanding. But we will never be willing to walk that path unless first we deal with our pride and choose to humble ourselves. As that wonderful Bible teacher Derek Prince used to say, *"the way down is the way up!"*

Prayer: *I am sorry, Lord, for any times I have despised myself and not benefited from godly correction when it was given. Help me, Lord, to listen carefully when You bring correction into my life. Help me to welcome it so that I may gain understanding and more fully walk in Your ways. In Jesus' Name, Amen.*

Personal Notes

Thank You LORD for the enquiry we received this week about one of the Finance roles at EG which, could only have been arranged by You & may Your Will be done in it all in Jesus Name. Amen!!!

Day 24 – 24/2/19

Eight Words that can Save Your Life!

"To fear the Lord is to hate evil." Proverbs 8:13

I've recently been casting my mind back over the years of Ellel Ministries and thinking of all the stories I would want to put in a book about what God has done since the work began back in 1986. As I did so, I found myself also thinking about some of the people we would love to have helped more than we were able – people for whom the key to their situation lay within the eight words of our short Scripture for today!

They were people who said they really loved the Lord. People who had been touched by Him at different times of their lives, but people, nevertheless, who were still struggling with issues that seemed to overwhelm them at regular intervals. They found that the temptations of the world were too often greater than they were able to handle and kept on slipping back into a variety of sinful behaviours, often of a sexual nature. Some came back several times – each time deeply repentant. But at the core of their being something serious was out of order, which made them prone to temptation and sin.

When talking about healing I often say that the best definition of healing that I know is *"the restoration of God's order in a person's life"*. This doesn't mean living life according to how I would like things to be, but living according to how God has said they should be. On this rock many people stumble. They want God to fit in with their ideas and desires – not the other way round! And at the end of the day, for some of these dear people, the real issue is not the size or the nature of their problem, but the simple fact that while they say they love the Lord, they haven't yet learned to hate evil!

Many times, I have written or spoken about the simple relationship there is between the fear of the Lord and love for the Lord. If you really love someone, you naturally don't want to do things that grieve them. And so it is, that if you REALLY love the Lord, the last thing you will ever want to do is to embrace any of the evil which separated man from God, and which Jesus died on the cross to set us free from.

If you are struggling with temptation of any form today, let's not be afraid to ask the hard question: have you fallen into the trap of loving this particular evil thing more than you love the Lord? If so, it may be time to repent – not so much of the sin associated with your problem, but of thinking it's OK not to hate evil, which is so often the real issue that underpins the problem of temptation! Loving evil will always separate us from God!

In the Lord's Prayer Jesus encouraged us to pray *"Deliver us from evil"*. However, the fact is God can't answer that prayer if we love evil more than we love Him.

Prayer: *Thank You, Lord, that You loved men and women such as me, so much, that You sent Jesus to die for our sins, in spite of the evil that separated You from mankind. Help me, Lord, to recognise evil when I see it, before it becomes a temptation and a trap I can fall into. Help me, also, Lord to hate evil and to choose to walk in the opposite direction when I am faced with ungodly choices. In Jesus' Name, Amen.*

Personal Notes

Thank You Heavenly Father for giving me the oppartunity to help lead the warship an this last weekend caurse, which I thoroughly enjayed and I praise Your Holy Name & exall You for all that You are daing in my life & in my Family's lives, in Jesus Name AMEN !!!
 I LOVE YOU & TRUST You, LORD !

Day 25 — 25/2/19

How Do You Receive a Rebuke?

"If you had responded to my rebuke, I would have poured out my heart to you and made my thoughts known to you." Proverbs 2:23

None of us likes to receive a rebuke. However, a rebuke given in love is like the lines of a railway, keeping the engine and the train on track and going in the right direction. But there is an enemy within, which each one of us has to contend with, which hates a rebuke from the Lord and does everything it possibly can to rise up in rejection of the loving advice which is implicit within a rebuke from the Lord. And the name of that enemy? Pride!

When pride is given control of our emotions and our reactions we put ourselves in a potentially dangerous place and, what is more, we miss out on all that God was waiting to pour into our hearts in order to bless, encourage

89

and direct our steps with His all-embracing love. He does not reject those He rebukes, for a rebuke from the Lord is a hallmark of His love (Hebrews 12:6).

A rebuke from the Lord, correctly received, opens the doors of our soul to the leading of the Spirit of God and knowing God`s thoughts for our lives. But He's not going to pour into our hearts all the things that He longs for us to understand, if as a result of our pride, we have given God the signal that we don't want to hear His voice.

In order to understand the ways of the Lord we have to learn to both recognise His voice when He speaks and respond gladly, even if what He says is a corrective rebuke. If we can learn to silence the voice of pride, and learn from the leading of the Lord, He will be constantly speaking His wisdom into our hearts, and our lives will be kept safely on track.

This is exactly what Jesus had to do with Simon Peter. Peter had been given extraordinary revelation about who Jesus was, *"the Messiah, the Son of the living God"* (Matthew 16:16). But when only a short while later, Jesus told the disciples that soon He would be killed, but that He would rise again on the third day, Simon Peter rose up to challenge what Jesus was saying. But in so doing, Peter was standing against the purposes of God for the salvation of the world.

There could only have been one source for such an idea and Jesus immediately recognised it and rebuked Peter with these unforgettable words, *"Get behind me, Satan! You are a stumbling block to me; you do not have in mind the concerns of God, but merely human concerns."* The rebuke was severe, but it was essential for Peter to know what the source was of his thinking. The rebuke was also part of the preparation that Jesus was putting Peter through for the great calling there was to be on his life.

I love the promise in ~~Hebrews~~ 1 Peter 5:6, 7 where God says *"Humble yourselves, therefore, under God's mighty hand, that he may lift you up in due time. Cast all your anxiety on him because he cares for you."* A rebuke from the Lord is an expression of His love and care. We need not fear it or be anxious – it is a sign that He is helping us step into His destiny for us, just as He did with Simon Peter.

Prayer: *I'm sorry, Lord, for the times when I have rejected Your loving rebuke into my life. Please forgive me for allowing pride to stand in the way of You pouring out Your heart into mine. I choose, Lord, to welcome Your rebuke whenever it`s necessary. Thank You, Lord, for Your care. In Jesus' Name, Amen.*

Personal Notes

Thank You Heavenly Father for Your Mercies (which are new every morning) & for Your Faithfulness which is great in our lives. Please help me to be humble before You & in my dealing with others in Jesus mighty Name. AMEN!!!

91

Day 26 - 26/2/19

Foolish Thinking

"A fool finds no pleasure in understanding but delights in airing his own opinions." Proverbs 18:2

A fool takes no interest or pleasure in either the truth that is written in God's Word or in the extraordinary evidence of a Creator in the creation that's all around us.

I was recently sitting on a headland, looking out to sea from a Scottish island as the sun slowly sank beneath the distant horizon. I was watching an incredible movie as minute by minute the wind, the waves, the sky and the sun danced to the Creator's baton as he conducted an orchestra of beauty and joy for our pleasure! In my heart I was marvelling at the Creator's genius and at the same time I was weeping because of the fools who see the same scene and have no understanding, but delight in their own opinions!

Science has not produced one shred of evidence to prove that God does not exist, and yet the absence of God from most of the educational curricula of the western world is powerful evidence that the opinions of atheistic man have now been adopted as fact by an unbelieving world. And once you have dispensed with the idea of God you also have to dispense with the laws of God – and right now the world is heading for a catastrophic brick wall as the consequences of dispensing with the laws of God become the suffering of mankind.

Oh, how God must weep when He sees mankind ignoring all the evidence deducible from His creation. The psalmist got it absolutely right when he said, *"The heavens declare the glory of God, the skies proclaim the work of his hands. Day after day they pour forth speech; night after night they display knowledge. There is no speech or language where their voice is not heard. Their voice goes out to the ends of the world"* (Psalm 19:1-4).

One day there will be a mighty revelation as the Judge of all the Earth comes to wind up the universe as we know it. When people see that happening, many will be like the foolish girls in Jesus' parable, rushing here and there trying to get oil in their lamps at the last minute, but it will be too late. *"For,"* said Paul, *"since the creation of the world God's invisible qualities, his eternal power and divine nature have been clearly seen, being understood from what has been made, so that men are without excuse"* (Romans 1:20) . . . *"Although they claimed to be wise, they became fools"* (Romans 1:22).

When man's pride makes him delight in the opinion of man at the expense of believing in Creator God, it is an expression of self-idolatry. And when man worships his own image, you can be sure that, ultimately, destruction will follow (Proverbs 16:18).

Prayer: *Thank You, Lord, for the incredible beauty of Your creation. Please forgive us, Lord, for the times when we have preferred to believe the opinions of man, rather than the truth written in Your Word and seen in Your creation. Open my eyes, Lord, to see You in everything that You have made. In Jesus' Name, Amen.*

Personal Notes

Day 27 – 27/2/19

Can You be Trusted to Deliver God's Message?

"A wicked messenger falls into trouble, but a trustworthy envoy brings healing." Proverbs 13:17

An envoy carries messages from the one who sends him. He is trusted by his employer to be a faithful carrier of the message, taking it to the person for whom it was intended. An envoy who fails to deliver the message, or who distorts the message, so that it is no longer the truth, will soon be in trouble, will lose their job and, in older days, would probably have lost their life as well! An envoy was trusted to be faithful to the one who sent him.

At the end of Matthew's Gospel, Jesus commissioned all His disciples to be His personal envoys and carry the message of the Gospel into all the world. Their role was not only to take the message, but to make more disciples, teaching all the new believers to do exactly the same things that He had taught those first disciples to do – which in Luke 9 verses 1 and 2 was clearly defined as to preach about the Kingdom of God, heal the sick and set people free from the powers of darkness.

A trustworthy envoy will not fail to do what he has been asked to do and as the writer of this proverb makes so very clear, the message of a trustworthy envoy will bring healing. And that's exactly what the Great Commission, which Jesus gave to the whole of the Church for the whole of time, does for those who receive the envoys' message and apply it in their lives.

Salvation is healing. Through the fall of man, death entered in to the human race, so we are all, literally, under sentence of death – not just physical death, but eternal spiritual death in total separation from the holy God who created us to love and be loved. When we are saved, we are born again to new life, which means we are raised from the dead (a very significant healing!). That means we no longer need fear the physical death which we are all heirs to, for we are already alive in Christ – both for time and eternity.

This is the message that Jesus told his envoys to declare to all who would listen. And then, as we apply the truths of salvation into our lives, God continues to bring His healing and wholeness into every area of our being.

God has entrusted His people to be His envoys – not just to tell people about the Gospel so that they will become believers, but so that they will also do the works of the Kingdom and become disciples as well. The Great Commission told us to make disciples – not just believers!

What a privilege it is to be sent by the living God, with the most incredible message that any envoy has ever been given – a message which has the capacity to transform the lives of those who receive and believe it. Are you willing to be a faithful envoy on behalf of the One who has sent you, to be a messenger of His truth and His love to the people Jesus died to save?

Prayer: *Help me, Lord, to be a faithful envoy and never to miss an opportunity to take the message of the Gospel to those who are in need of Your healing and Your salvation. In Jesus' name, Amen.*

Personal Notes — 28/2/19

Thank You LORD for bringing the people You wanted here for fellowship at our home here at Ashley Gardens yesterday evening. Everyone felt relaxed & friendly which made it an enjoyable time. Thank You LORD for Your presence with us & for Your protection & Peace. AMEN !!!

Day 28 – 28/2/19

The Harvest of Work

"He who works his land will have abundant food, but he who chases fantasies lacks judgment." Proverbs 12:11

This proverb comes from the days when each and every family worked their own land in order to grow crops and produce food that would sustain them throughout the year. Land does not produce anything by itself. An abundant harvest requires time and effort to first prepare the ground by ploughing and nourishing the ground with manure or fertiliser. It then has to be carefully prepared for sowing the seed, followed by regular watering.

All of this represents hard work – but the rewards at harvest-time are great. A farmer who just sowed the seed on unploughed ground, hoping for a good crop, would have very little to harvest at the end of the growing season. His laziness would result in his family going hungry.

Most of us are not able to work land in order to feed our families, but there is still a profound lesson for each and every one of us in today's Scripture. God has given us all gifts and abilities – gifts and abilities which we can use to meet the needs of other people and thereby earn a living. It's no use praying for God to meet our needs if, at the same time, we are failing to *"work the land of our lives"*. That is chasing fantasies! Wages don't fall off trees, they are earned.

But there is a different kind of harvest about which Jesus was very concerned. We can certainly pray for those in our community who don't know the Lord, but if we do nothing to plough and nourish the land' by building relationship with them, our prayers will be limited in their effectiveness. It was when Jesus met and talked with the woman at the well and shared with her about the water of life that she was changed for ever.

A man worked for me for many years. Whenever opportunity offered I would share with him about the Lord. He became a good friend, but he had seen bad things in the war and his heart was hardened towards God. But he couldn't ignore some of the things that God had done in the business I ran. God was preparing him for salvation. I ploughed his land, sowed seed and then, one day he had a heart attack and was critically ill. As I sat with him in hospital, he was finally ready to open his heart to God. There was a harvest on Earth and rejoicing in Heaven that night. The following day he died. Now I'm looking forward to seeing him again!

We need to work the land of our lives and be always alert to the potential of every personal encounter, so that we can build bridges into the lives of those who are in need of salvation. God so encouraged me in this respect through the words of the prophet Haggai, who said *"Work, for I am with you, says the Lord of Hosts"* (Haggai 2:4).

Prayer: *Help me, Lord, to always use the gifts You have given me to earn the bread that we need for nourishment. But help us, too, Lord, to farm the land of our community and seek to produce a harvest for Your Kingdom of lives that have been changed by Your presence and saved for eternity. In Jesus' name, Amen.*

Personal Notes

Thank You Heavenly Father
for giving me a heart for
the people in my community
especially my neighbours to
be saved & to come to know
our LORD Jesus Christ as their
personal LORD & saviour.
Teach us to hear You clearly
about how to reach out to
our neighbours with the Gospel
in love, in Jesus Name &
to Your Glory. AMEN!
I am also concerned about
Ismail but I know You are
watching over Him. AMEN!!!

Day 29 – 1/3/19

ALWAYS!

"Blessed is the man who always fears the Lord, but he who hardens his heart falls into trouble." Proverbs 28:14

There are many scriptures which encourage people to live with a holy fear of the Lord, but there is one word in our verse for today which sets this particular scripture apart from all the others – it's the word *always*.

Always is a word which doesn't allow for any variation in standard or practice – it simply means, in this context, that whenever you face a choice or a decision in which you have an opportunity to either obey the Lord, or to sin, then you don't even have to think about it. The decision in your heart has already been made – you will ALWAYS allow fear of the Lord to determine your actions. The last thing you would ever want to do is grieve the Lord. The peace of God will always follow the decisions you make when they take into account God's perspective before you consider your own – that's what it can mean to fear the Lord.

The second part of the verse explains how it is that people can choose to ignore the Lord and even though they know something is wrong, go ahead and do it. They have to harden their heart – and to harden one's heart and go against God is not a good idea! There are many stories in the Bible which tell of what happened when people knowingly chose to harden their hearts and oppose God. This happened many times with the people of Israel in their wilderness years after fleeing Egypt.

Hebrews 3:7-11 speaks directly into our own lives when the writer uses those experiences of the children of Israel to warn us of the dangers of hardening our hearts. When they hardened their hearts, they invoked the anger of God.

So, verse 8 brings the Scripture right up to date. This is not something which is confined to the history books, it's relevant here and now to teach every one of us, 24/7: *"Today, if you hear his voice, do not harden your hearts."* Which simply means, when God speaks, listen. And when you've heard, obey!

My great Uncle Will used to say *"Never sit on a spiritual urge"* which, in his home-spun language meant *"What are you waiting for? Get on with it."* I've never forgotten him saying those simple but very profound words. And I've always sought to 'get on with it' whenever I sensed a spiritual urge from the Lord. I can look back now and say that some of the most important and significant events in my life came about because of doing what Uncle Will had taught me. Samuel put it this way when he had to go and correct King Saul, *"obedience is better than sacrifice"* (1 Samuel 15:22).

A hardened heart is very dangerous. Our conscience becomes dimmed and we become less and less sensitive to the leading of the Holy Spirit. And the more we go our own way, the harder the heart becomes and, as our Scripture tells us, there will be trouble ahead. The word 'always' is an absolute antidote to a hardened heart. Allow holy fear to keep your life on God's track and ALWAYS make your decisions in the fear of the Lord.

Prayer: *Help me, Lord, to remember the importance of the word 'always'. I recognise that Satan will constantly want to trip me up and I choose now to live in the fear of the Lord and not to harden my heart. Thank You for the promise of the peace of God which will then always be in my heart. In Jesus' Name, Amen.*

Personal Notes

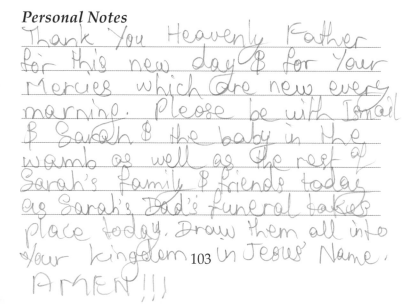

Thank You Heavenly Father for this new day & for Your Mercies which are new every morning. Please be with Ismael & Sarah & the baby in the womb as well as the rest of Sarah's family & friends today as Sarah's Dad's funeral takes place today. Draw them all into Your kingdom in Jesus' Name. AMEN!!!

103

Day 30 – 2/3/19

Learning Life's Lessons – God's Way!

"Train a child in the way that he should go, and when he is old he will not depart from it." Proverbs 22:6

M
argaret Thatcher was Britain's longest serving Prime Minister in the twentieth century. There will be few reading this who haven't heard of her. The great and famous of the nation, together with Her Majesty the Queen and the Duke of Edinburgh, were present at St.Paul's Cathedral for her funeral service.

Margaret Thatcher was known as a strong leader and she had a deeply entrenched respect for the laws of God. But where did that come from? It came from her childhood upbringing. Her father, a Methodist lay-preacher would take her Sunday by Sunday to churches all over Lincolnshire, where she heard him preach from the Word of God. God's Word became her childhood meat and drink. While studying Chemistry, and then Law, at Oxford University she herself became a Methodist lay preacher. Her sermon on *"Seek ye first the Kingdom of God"* was described as outstanding. And she took prayer meetings "extremely seriously".

Famous people sometimes have the privilege of preparing the Order of Service for their own funeral. Margaret Thatcher was known for her great attention to detail, so she carefully prepared instructions for how the event should be conducted. She specifically asked that there be no political eulogy at the service, because, she said, *"the sole object of worship must be God!"*

And then she asked that the Prime Minister of the day should read the second lesson, carefully chosen by herself from John's Gospel. So, at her funeral service, David Cameron, the Prime Minister, read to the world from John 14:1-6, which begins with the words, *"Do not let your hearts be troubled. Trust in God"* and concludes with Jesus answering Thomas's profound question, *"How can we know the way"* by saying, *"I am the way and the truth and the life. No-one comes to the Father except through me."*

So where did the 87-year old lady learn such wisdom? As our Scripture for the day reminds us, it came from her childhood upbringing. When she became old, she did not depart from what she learned about God from her father's preaching, and her childhood upbringing in the heart of her local Methodist Church.

As a child I, too, went with my Dad on many occasions when he was preaching at Methodist, and other denominational Chapels. I sat through Dad's preaching and his ministry from the Word of God imperceptibly soaked into my spirit. I was so privileged to be blessed in this way.

What a privilege it is for us all to impart a knowledge of God to the next generations. None of us knows what fruit there will be in the generations yet to come. I pray that we will each take seriously our own personal responsibility to impact the generations yet to come with the truth that Jesus is the only way!

Prayer: *Thank You, Lord, for those who have impacted my life with truth from the Word of God. Help me, Lord, to serve You and the generations yet to come, by sharing my knowledge of You with those who are young, so that when they are old, they will still desire to serve You. In Jesus' Name, Amen.*

Personal Notes – 3/3/18

Thank You LORD for seeing me through this week with all the work that needs to be done + the Explore B work and for giving me peace & good health through it all. All the glory, honour, wisdom, praise, thanksgiving power & strength/might belong to You for ever & ever. AMEN!!!

Day 31 – 3/3/19

Wounds that Bring Healing!

"Wounds from a friend can be trusted, but an enemy multiplies kisses." Proverbs 27:6

When someone you know, love and trust, takes the huge risk of sharing something difficult with you, it may be hard for you to receive and even be hurtful, like a wound. Their words may penetrate your defences and you feel the pain. But such wounds can be life-changing and life-giving, especially when they come from someone with a pure heart and no ulterior motive.

There are times in my own life when friends with a genuine and rightful concern have come to talk with me – sometimes with a real issue that I have then had to take to the Lord; and at other times for clarification of something they didn't understand. But when you know their heart you need not fear their motive.

Conversely, when someone flatters you with nice words, especially if they seem 'over the top', even too good to be true, you are right to be suspicious. Their words could be like the *"multiplied kisses of an enemy"*. You begin to suspect an ulterior motive and then wonder what it is that they are wanting from you. No-one likes to be patronised like this with deceptive words. Proverbs 29:5 expresses it this way, *"Whoever flatters his neighbour is spreading a net for his feet."*

However, because we all like to have nice things said about us, carefully engineered flattery can sometimes make us lower our guard and become vulnerable to making serious mistakes. It could potentially trap us into doing something that can have unfortunate, even dangerous, consequences in our lives.

There are many times when people have come for prayer about something in their life and instead of praying about their presenting symptoms, I have had to challenge them about something that was out of order. Often it was something they were trying to hide below the surface of their life but which, in reality, was at the very root of their superficial problem. They needed to hear the words of a faithful friend, even though, at first, it may have felt like a wound.

Sometimes, in circumstances like this, the initial response is anger, before they come to the point of recognising the truth that they are having to face. It's not easy to confront people over what are often very sensitive issues, but if you don't, you run the danger of missing a golden opportunity to help them get right with God. Proverbs 28:23 neatly sums this up by saying, *"He who rebukes a man will in the end gain more favour than he who has a flattering tongue."*

When the rich young ruler came to Jesus and asked *"what good thing must I do to get eternal life?"* (Matthew 19:16), he may have been expecting a flattering compliment from Jesus for asking such a good question! But Jesus looked right through him and touched the idol in his heart when He said, *"Go, sell your possessions and give to the poor and you will have treasure in heaven. Then come follow me"* (Matthew 19:21). The reality for this man was that his wealth was more important to him than following Jesus!

There can be many things which have become idols in our hearts and when a friend, in love, has the courage to come and touch that thing, we may be initially angry at what they are saying and feel wounded. But if we open our ears to listen to what God is saying to us, then such painful encounters can prove to be the most important and healing days of our life!

Prayer: *Thank You, Lord, that You care enough about each one of us to confront us with the truth. I pray that, just as You spoke to the rich young ruler, You will speak clearly to me about anything that is out of order in my life. Show me from Your Word or through someone You send to me. Help me not to reject wounds that will bring healing to me, nor to be deceived by flattery. In Jesus' Name, Amen.*

Personal Notes – 4/3/19

Thank You LORD for Your
Word that says:
"You have not given us a
spirit of fear but of power
& of Love & of a sound mind."
and your Word that says:
" All your children will be
taught by the LORD and great
will be their peace"
and Your Word that also says:
".... I will contend with those
who contend with you and
your children I will save"
AMEN, AMEN & AMEN!!!

Day 32 – 4/3/19

The Power of Wisdom

"By wisdom a house is built, and through understanding it is established; through knowledge its rooms are filled with rare and beautiful treasures. A wise man has great power, and a man of knowledge increases in strength." (Proverbs 24:3-5)

Power and authority are not the same thing. A person in authority uses power to carry out ~~what~~ whatever it is he has to do. A boxer has power in his muscles but he only has authority to use it in the boxing ring against an opponent. It's the boxing ring that gives him his authority – and it is only here that he can use his power.

Power has the capacity to be a huge blessing or a terrible curse. The power of a railway engine can transport people across the land in comfort. But if that same engine, at the height of its power, leaves the track at speed, there would be a terrible disaster. The power of a wise ruler with a good government can be a huge blessing to the people of a nation. But a despotic ruler who has no other objective than to use his power to control other people and satisfy his own objectives, is a curse upon the nations.

Now, the privilege of being the ruler of a nation is reserved for only a very few people, but these principles can apply to each and every one of us. For we are all capable of acting with love and generosity towards those who are under our authority or treating them with harshness and cruelty.

I will never forget the lady who almost spat at me, when I encouraged her to trust God as her Father. Eventually, through her pain and anger, she told me how her father would beat her, and her brothers and sisters, every night when he came home from the pub, drunk. *"I know what fathers are like and if that's what God's like, I don't want to know him!"* she said.

Her father's wrong use of power in the family had caused her terrible pain and a life of suffering. Some people use the power they have to inflict suffering on the people they control, so as to make them do what they want out of fear. A harsh boss at work can keep people under control through his temper and bad language. And tragically we have had to pray with many people who were abused at home, physically, verbally or sexually, by those who wrongfully used the authority that they had in the family over their children.

Our Scripture for today paints a very different picture, however. It's a picture of a person who has gained knowledge and wisdom in life and, as a result, is making wise and profitable decisions and has become powerful in the community, but only uses his power for good. I will never cease to be thankful to God for wise parents who exercised their authority in the family firmly and with much love. They taught me so much and I will be eternally grateful to them.

The good news for those who have suffered under a harsh authority, wherever that may have been, is that Jesus came to show us what the Father is really like. God is not an abusive Father. His arms of love are always open for the hurting and the broken, for those who have suffered the cruelty of abuse of power. This is the message that God gave through Isaiah to the world in Isaiah 61:1-3. The Messiah was coming to *"heal the broken-hearted and set the captives free"*. And there is forgiveness for those who know they have used their powers abusively and cruelly.

Prayer. *Help me, Lord, to forgive those who have abused their power and hurt me at different times of my life. Then help me, Lord, to always use the power that You have given me in every sphere of life with love and wisdom. Help me never to take advantage of those who are under my authority. And thank You, Jesus, that even though all authority has been give into Your hands that You are still the Good Shepherd who loves and cares for Your sheep – even me! In Jesus' Name, Amen*

Personal Note

Thank You Heavenly Father
for Your amazing Love
for me & my Family
– Seny, Ismail, Ferida
& Rashid – and stand on
Your Faithful Ward that
You will never leave us
nor forsake us, in Jesus
Mighty Name. AMEN!!!

Day 33 – 5/3/19

How to Prosper

"Whoever gives heed to instruction prospers, and blessed is he who trusts in the Lord." Proverbs 16:20

One of the reasons why 'pride goes before destruction' is that pride tends to make people unteachable. They think they know it all – and don't want anyone else to tell them what to do or bring any form of instruction or correction into their life. They know best and that's that!

But, sadly, that means that they can never learn from other people and they condemn themselves to making mistake after mistake, because they are never willing to listen to the wisdom of others. This is especially true about learning the ways of the Lord, and being willing to listen to His instruction. It is not for nothing that the most sung song of the twentieth century was Frank Sinatra's *"My way"*. Supreme arrogance and pride is represented by the lyrics, which talk about facing the final curtain (death) and saying (presumably to God) that I did it my way!

Humility is the opposite of pride. And a humble person, who is keen to learn, will grow in knowledge and understanding, learning from others and equipping themselves for life. A person who loves, respects and listens to the Lord is said to fear the Lord, knowing that what God has said will always be the truth and that when we follow Jesus, who is *"the Way, the Truth and the Life"* then we will be best equipped for living our own life, whatever the circumstances are that we have to face or live through.

It's no surprise that there are many places in God's Word which encourage us to live our lives in the fear of the Lord. Exodus 20:20, for example, tells us that *"the fear of God with you, will keep you from sinning."* But my favourite verse about the fear of the Lord is Psalm 25:14, where we read that *"The Lord confides in those who fear him."*

It's wonderful news to hear that God confides in those that fear Him. For that simply means that God will speak directly into our lives by His Spirit, or through His Word, showing us what He wants us to do and the way to go!

Isaiah tells it this way, *"your ears will hear a voice behind you, saying, 'This is the way, walk in it'"* (Isaiah 30:21). The most costly mistakes I made in my own life were when I decided to ignore God's voice or silence my conscience. The result was always painful. Yes, there is forgiveness for sin, but, isn't it oh so much better not to have stepped out of God's way in the first place?

It is also a fact that in my own business life, the most successful and prosperous decisions were those which were clearly made in obedience to the direction the Lord had told me to go. Ideas God gave me in specific answer to prayer, were those which were the most successful. One business decision I made forty years ago was instrumental in providing financial support in over thirty years of ministry. God is the best businessman I know, and He delights to confide in us.

When we have learnt to trust the Lord, we will not hesitate to be obedient to His Word and do those things that please Him. And, as Proverbs 1:33 expresses it, *"Whoever listens to me will live in safety and be at ease without fear or harm."*

Prayer: *Forgive me, Lord, for those times in my life when, through pride, I have tried to do it my way and failed to take wise instruction. But thank You, Lord, that You have promised to guide and direct the steps of those who truly love and fear You. Help me, Lord, to be always attentive to Your voice and not to wander off the pathway that You lay before me. In Jesus' Name, Amen.*

Personal Notes – 6/3/19

Thank You LORD for the gifts of Life & Love and also for the gifts of family & children as well as the amazing joy of being a member of Your Family/Household/Kingdom. AMEN!

Day 34 — 6/3/19

Guard Your Heart

"Above all else, guard your heart, for it is the wellspring of life." Proverbs 4:23

A wellspring is the place where something important comes from. It is the source of a stream and then a river. It's where things begin. And our Scripture for today tells us that our heart is a wellspring, the very centre of our being, the wellspring of life.

The heart being talked of here is not our physical blood-pump, but the very core of our being. It is, therefore, absolutely central to who we are as a person. It's where our thoughts, feelings and emotions come together and express themselves and influence the will choices that we make. It is, therefore, of critical importance. No wonder we are told here to guard our heart. For if we don't we will be vulnerable to influences from every possible direction and to the temptations which the enemy may put before us.

Hebrews 4:12 tells us that it is the thoughts and the attitudes of our heart that are judged by the living and active Word of God, described here as being sharper than any double-edged sword. It's as if the Word of God becomes the straight edge, or plumb line, against which the choices we make are measured. For when the motives of our heart are out of tune with God, we are in danger and heading for trouble.

Paul warns us to be very careful what we think about. He encourages us *"to take captive every thought and make it obedient to Christ"* (2 Corinthians 10:5). For the ungodly things we dwell on in our minds penetrate the defences of our heart and we can then become vulnerable to putting those thoughts into action – and so a cycle of ungodly thinking motivates the heart and leads us into ungodly actions.

These actions then, in turn, store up ungodly memories for the mind to dwell on, thus feeding a cycle which can dominate and control and become the root of addictions and addictive behaviour. This is serious stuff!

How precious it is when a child comes to faith in Jesus when they are young, before their mind and their heart have been challenged by the degrading standards that are prevalent in the moral behaviour of the adult world. The sooner their heart is turned towards the Lord, the easier it will be, as they grow and mature, to maintain a pure heart and guard the wellspring of life within them.

Satan would want our heart to be polluted by ungodly desires. But Paul in his letter to the Philippians urged believers to counter the enemy's inroads by thinking on *"whatever is true, whatever is noble, whatever is right, whatever is pure, whatever is lovely and whatever is admirable"* (Philippians 4:8). By so doing, Paul was giving very practical advice on how to guard our hearts as we are urged to do by today's Scripture.

Prayer: *Thank You, Jesus, that with You as the Lord of my life, I can keep my heart pure. Help me to resist the temptations of the enemy and guard my heart, so that Satan is not able to blow my life off course and rob me of my destiny in God. In Jesus' Name, Amen.*

Personal Notes

Thank You Heavenly Father for this New day that You have made & may we rejoice & be glad in it as it is the day that You blessed our family with a beautiful boy — Rashid, who we love so much but we also know that You love him much more than we can ever love him, and that You have a plan for his life that will bring glory to Your Holy Name in Jesus' Christ. AMEN!!!

What You See Is What You Get! WYSIWYG

"For whoever finds me finds life and receives favour from the Lord. But whoever fails to find me harms himself; all who hate me love death." Proverbs 8:35 and 36

WYG is a popular computing acronym which simply means *'What You See Is What You Get'*. But it has also assumed a meaning beyond the world of computing to describe a person whose character is transparent and exemplary, with no hidden or unpleasant characteristics. How the person is seen to behave is an exact representation of the true character of the individual. Another way of putting it is that they are the 'same all the way through' – which means that they have integrity.

While the acronym WYSIWYG was completely unknown in Solomon's day, the principle that this acronym stands for was definitely not unknown. In Proverbs 6:16-19, for example, we read of things that the Lord hates, three of which are a lying tongue, a heart that devises wicked schemes, and a false witness who pours out lies.

A person may want to give the impression that they are pure and truthful. But if in their heart they are devising evil things and lies they can tell, then what people see on the outside is definitely not the same as what they are like on the inside. God hates it when mankind, who was made by God in the image and likeness of their Creator, behaves in a way that is contrary to His character.

But the fact is that every single one of us carries the stain of sin in our hearts which God hates. In reality, none of us can say that we are 100% WYSIWYGs! Our sin can be forgiven because of what Jesus did for us on the cross, but this side of Heaven the sin seed, with all its evil potential, is always in our hearts. This is often described as our carnal nature, meaning that we will always fail the WYSIWYG test!

But that's not true of God. When Jesus walked this earth what people saw on the outside was always a true reflection of the inside. He was without sin and at all times He was a pure, 100% clean representative of His Father, God. And the crucial difference between Jesus and every other human being was that because of sin all of mankind is under the curse of death. But sinless Jesus was the bringer of life – life in all its fulness.

Only Jesus could have said those amazing words from John 14:6, *"I am the way, the truth and the life."* For only He is the way to the Father. Only His lips spoke total truth. And only He could be the bringer of life into a world that was under the sentence of death. When people met Jesus, what they saw really was what they got! When they heard Jesus speak, they heard what God the Father would say. And in verse 9 of John 14 Jesus said, *"Anyone who has seen me has seen the Father."*

So, when we read in our Scripture for today that *"whoever finds Me (God), finds life"*, we are reading the truth that was vitally important to people of that day, but we are also reading a prophetic truth about Jesus which is relevant to us here and now – whoever finds Him, finds life! He is not a deceiver, His teaching won't ever disappoint, His words will never turn out to be lies, Hs promises will never let you down. In Jesus what you see is exactly what you get!

Prayer: Thank You, Jesus, that You faithfully represented Father God to a fallen and broken world. Your Word promises that if we truly seek You we will surely find You. And when we find You, we will find life – resurrection life – life from the dead. Help me, Lord, never to forget who You are, where you came from and that one day I will be together with You in Heaven. In Jesus' Name. Amen.

Personal Notes – 8/3/19

Thank You LORD that You got Ismail to contact me yesterday as he needed information from me, and that He is beginning to share some of his deepest feeling (e.g. of shame). May Your amazing love & glorious divine Light shine through the cloak of shame around him in Jesus Name to disperse it forever. AMEN!!!

123

Day 36 – 8/3/19

Spiritual Laziness

"I went past the field of the sluggard, past the vineyard of the man who lacks judgment; thorns had come up everywhere, the ground was covered with weeds, and the stone wall was in ruins. I applied my heart to what I observed and learned a lesson from what I saw: A little sleep, a little slumber, a little folding of the hands to rest – and poverty will come on you like a bandit and scarcity like an armed man." Proverbs 24:30-34

The Bible is full of parables – from beginning to end. We ignore them at our peril! This one speaks very directly to the sin of laziness and the writer reaches the correct conclusion from what he saw – that the man who sleeps when he should have been working will soon end up in poverty. This message is obvious, the advice in the message is life-saving.

In the work that we do, however, we come across many people who may have been very diligent in working for money but have been careless about the way they have lived their lives. They have known that there were issues they needed to address, but they have allowed the 'weeds' to grow and their sensitivity towards the voice of God has been dulled. Their spiritual defences (the walls of their heart) have been broken down, and oftentimes the enemy has gained access. By responding only to the physical pressures of life, they have ignored the obvious spiritual signs of danger and carried on regardless.

They have said to themselves – one day, I'll get to it! But, spiritually, they have behaved like the sluggard in the parable who never attended to the essentials when caring for his vineyard. Just as surely as the physically lazy man will end up in poverty, the spiritually lazy person will soon become vulnerable – not to armed bandits, but something much worse! For, as Peter tells us so graphically, in 1 Peter 5:8, *"the enemy prowls around like a roaring lion, looking for someone to devour"*.

One of my saddest experiences was listening to the grief of an old man who had known there were things wrong with his life when he was young and had ignored the call of God to love and serve Him. He told himself that he was too busy and too committed in the family business and that he would answer God's call when he had more time. For now, God would have to wait. In his thirties God spoke to him again, And then in his forties and his fifties. But then God ceased to speak. As an old man he was heart-broken at his own spiritual laziness, that had robbed him of God's best for his life. He repented and no doubt he received forgiveness – but his life was devoid of the fruit that God had planned for him. God had been robbed also.

Let us not follow the example of the 'vineyard sluggard' but choose now to get out of our spiritual armchairs and tackle any vital issues we have been putting off, before it's too late.

Prayer: *Thank You, Lord, that Your word reminds me of the need to be diligent in the 'vineyard of my life'. Help me to see where the weeds are growing and the walls are broken down and do something about them without delay. In Jesus' name, Amen.*

Personal Notes

Thank You Heavenly Father for this new day that You have made, help us to rejoice & be glad in it as Your mercies are new every morning that Your Most Holy Name will be glorified in our lives in our families & in all that we do in Jesus Mighty Name. AMEN!! May Peace reign everywhere You put us today. Hallelujah!! Amen!!

Day 37 – 9/3/19

Beware the Dangers of Beer and Wine!

"Wine is a mocker and beer is a brawler; whoever is led astray by them is not wise." Proverbs 20:1. *"Do not gaze at wine when it is red, when it sparkles in the cup, when it goes down smoothly. In the end it bites like a snake and poisons like a viper."* Proverbs 23:31-32

The arguments about whether or not a Christian should drink alcohol have divided believers down the centuries. It is true that the Bible doesn't say anywhere that it is a sin to drink alcohol. There is no doubt that Jesus turned the water into the best wine at the wedding banquet. And there are no grounds for thinking that the wine that was used at the last supper was not real wine. But the Bible is also very straight about the inherent dangers of drinking more wine and beer than is good for you. Scriptures such as these cannot be ignored.

No-one would dispute that alcohol-fuelled behaviour is an ungodly curse on society. When people begin to lose control of their tongue and their senses they become vulnerable to every possible kind of temptation and their behaviour can become obnoxious and aggressive. The courts are constantly hearing cases of sexual assault and violent behaviour under the influence of alcohol, which have wreaked havoc on people's lives, causing terrible suffering. Countless abortions have followed alcohol-inspired sexual activity.

And right across the world, driving under the influence of alcohol claims thousands of lives. In the UK, on average, 3,000 people are killed or seriously injured every year from drink-drive accidents. In the USA thirty people die every single day – that's about 11,000 deaths a year. These are astonishing and terrible statistics.

It's not surprising, therefore, that God has placed many warnings in the Bible about the potential spiritual and physical dangers of excess drinking – we ignore them at our peril. And medical science is now backing up Scripture with well-substantiated health warnings that even modest levels of alcohol consumption can significantly cut life expectancy!

The Bible is making a serious point when it says that in the end wine *"bites like a snake and poisons like a viper"*. As Christians we should not only listen to these warnings in

Scripture, but also take note of what medical science is now telling us. The long-term consequence of drinking more than is good for us could be robbing us, our families and God of years of our life, and also induce years of disease-related suffering. And we should be doubly determined never to touch alcohol if we are about to drive a car.

The body God has given us is precious. It is our responsibility to look after it. Paul says *"your body is a temple of the Holy Spirit, who is in you, whom you have received from God. You are not your own, you were bought with a price. Therefore, honour God with your body"* (1 Corinthians 6:19).

So, as believers, we know that our whole life is precious to God and that every hour, yes even every minute, matters to Him. Looking after the body, therefore, is a deeply spiritual responsibility and today's Scripture should act as an alarm call to make us review how much we do drink, and how we treat the body God has given us, so that we can remain fit for His service for all the years that God had planned for us.

Prayer: *Thank You, Lord, for the body You have given me and all the things You have created for our enjoyment. Forgive me, Lord, for any way in which I have abused my body by drinking more than is wise. I want to live all the years you had planned for me. Help me, I pray, to be self-disciplined as I seek to serve You with everything I am. In Jesus' Name, Amen.*

Personal Notes

God's Recipe for Good Health

"Do not be wise in your own eyes, fear the Lord and shun evil. This will bring health to your body and nourishment to your bones." Proverbs 3:7-8

As we have now discovered, there are many sayings in the book of Proverbs which link the fear of the Lord with godly living. One leads to the other. But this proverb takes the principle a very significant step further. It's saying that there can be a definite link between our behaviour and our health.

There are three steps to wholeness explicit within these sayings. The first is simply a recognition that the wisdom of God is more important than the supposed wisdom of man. We can make assessments of a situation and, even though our conclusion is different from what God has said in His Word, if we decide that we know better than God, we are being wise in our own eyes.

A good example of this in today's amoral world is having sexual relations before marriage. The world says it's OK – and almost everyone does it. Even, sadly, many believers who, instead of being salt and light in the world, have brought the darkness of the world into the church. Man, supposedly, knows best and now that we have reliable contraception, "why not?", people say. If you do not understand that when man and woman are joined together in sex that they become part of each other – and both are now different people than they were before the relationship occurred, you will not have any understanding as to what the consequences might be.

 It is only fear of the Lord that will keep people from sinning (Exodus 20:20) and give us the courage and wisdom to avoid evil – not just the evil that man might consider to be bad, but what God defines as being evil (sinful) in His Word.

By shunning those things that God defines as evil, we avoid walking on Satan's territory. If you walk through mud, your shoes will carry the stain onto the carpet when you go into your house. If we walk on Satan's turf we will carry the stain of sin, and sometimes the powers of darkness as well, into our inner being, even our body which should, as described by Paul, only be *"a temple of the Holy Spirit"* (1 Corinthians 6:19).

We can now see how the health of our body can be affected by the consequences of not avoiding evil. This helps us to understand how it is that sometimes people are physically healed through repentance and deliverance. For when a spirit which has brought infirmity into the body is driven out, then healing can follow – something that I have seen on many occasions as we have prayed for God to deliver and heal. These important principles are carefully taught and illustrated in my book *Healing Through Deliverance* (*Sovereign World* and *Chosen*). James, also, was very explicit about these matters when he said, *"confess your sins to each other and pray for each other so that you may be healed"* (James 5:16).

So, there is not only an eternal spiritual benefit of living a godly life, there is also the temporal physical promise of good health. I am sure that when Solomon wrote these words, he had no idea that the blood is made in the bones. But the knowledge and wisdom of God was in what he was inspired to write. We read in Scripture that *"life is in the blood"* (Leviticus 17:11) and now, also, have the knowledge of medical science, so we can more fully understand the significance of these words. Healthy blood leads to a healthy life. If our bones are being nourished, then our whole being is being blessed!

Prayer: *Thank You, Lord, for the detail that You have placed in Your Word. I am sorry for the times when I have not avoided evil and I have suffered as a result. I pray that You will forgive and cleanse me, so that I may be free to be healed. In Jesus' Name, Amen.*

Personal Notes

Day 39 — 11/3/19

Truth and Integrity – the Keys to a Successful Life

"The integrity of the upright guides them, but the unfaithful are destroyed because of their duplicity."
Proverbs 11:3

As we come towards the end of our 40-day devotional journey, I am wanting to look at how it's possible to walk into the future with both faith and confidence.

There are some key words in today's Scripture – integrity, upright and duplicity. These words will help us understand the principles involved. Integrity means that you are the same all the way through. Upright means that you choose to live your life according to God's Word and His laws, not your own good ideas. But duplicity means being two-faced, dishonest and deceitful.

If a person is two-faced, it means that they are presenting one side of their character or personality to one party and another side to a different party. They can be saying one thing but thinking another. They can be flattering you with their words but despising you with their thoughts.

And in terms of our relationship to God, it means that on the outside we are giving the impression that we love the Lord and want to serve Him at all times, but that the inner motives of our heart are very different. We then become unbalanced and it is not surprising, therefore, that it says in James 1:8 that *"a double-minded man is unstable in all his ways."* An unstable and unbalanced person is a danger to themselves and to anyone who chooses to depend on them.

The saddest form of spiritual duplicity is when people swallow their own lie and try to deceive themselves. They can believe one thing but, in reality, the truth about themselves is very different from the image they present. They can use this false image to try and manipulate others and even try and manipulate God! It's sometimes not easy to see what is going on – even in our own hearts. We need to ask the Holy Spirit to truly reflect back to us the picture of us that He sees, so that we can become single-minded and not be vulnerable to being imbalanced.

The words integrity and upright are easier to understand. An upright person is not only one who follows and obeys the Lord, but one on whom you can trust not to change their behaviour or beliefs to suit their circumstances and impress whoever they happen to be with. A person with integrity is someone on whom you can trust to always be the same in their beliefs, reactions and behaviour. So, a person who is upright has integrity, and you know that they can be totally depended on. That is the sort of person we need to become and remain before God – so that He can always depend on us to not only walk in His ways, but to do His Kingdom works. We won't then fall into the deadly traps of unfaithfulness caused by duplicity.

It's an exciting but awesome thought, that God depends on us to be true to ourselves and true to Him. When you look at Christian history, these are the people on whom God has depended to do His work. They could be depended on to act with integrity and be upright in all their dealings, so God trusted them.

So, do you want to be unfaithful, with duplicity as a hallmark of your character? Or do you want to be faithful and live an upright life of truth and integrity. You can be sure that if your heart's desire is the latter that God will rejoice to be at your side to help you in all the stages of life's journey. Proverbs 13:6 tells us that *"Righteousness guards the person of integrity."* And Proverbs 4:18 tells us that, *"The path of the righteous is like the morning sun, shining ever brighter till the full light of day."*

Prayer: *Thank You, Lord Jesus, that in everything You said and did You acted with truth and integrity and that, as a result, we can unconditionally depend on You. Help me, Lord, to so live that there is no duplicity in my heart so that You can depend on me to always be available to do whatever You want me to do. In Jesus' Name, Amen.*

Personal Notes

Day 40 — 12/3/19

"My Words . . . are Life . . . and Health"

"Listen, my son, accept what I say, and the years of your life will be many. I instruct you in the way of wisdom and lead you along straight paths. When you walk, your steps will not be hampered; when you run, you will not stumble. Hold on to instruction, do not let it go; guard it well, for it is your life." Proverbs 4:10-13

The first few chapters of the book of Proverbs are written as if Wisdom herself is speaking. The name Wisdom represents the Holy Spirit of God – for in Him is all truth, all knowledge and all wisdom. We read how Wisdom invites sinful man to learn of God, and through the application of wisdom be challenged, be encouraged, be rebuked, be corrected, be inspired, be healthy, be guided – and many more things which are expressed through the thirty-one chapters of this remarkable book.

For this, our final devotion, we come to a very simple instruction – an instruction from Wisdom that, if followed, will have massive consequences for each and every one of us – *"Accept what I say"*. This is an instruction which can, literally, make the difference between life and death. Do we or do we not believe that what God says is true and that if we follow and obey Him it will be life-saving, life-giving and life-fulfilling?

I once saved the life of a terrified young boy whose canoe had capsized in a raging torrent of flood water. He was stranded on a rock in the middle of the river above a dangerous and very deep weir. I managed to cast my fishing line around his legs. Then I tied string to the fishing line which he dragged to himself. And finally I found a rope in a farmer's barn which I attached to the string. Even though he now had a rope tied round his waist, the force of the water was too strong for me to pull him up-stream away from the weir. To be saved, he was going to have to step into the raging torrent pouring over the edge of the weir and trust that I could pull the rope hard and fast enough across the surface to prevent him from being sucked under. This dangerous manoeuvre would only work if he accepted what I told him to do, held on tight, jumped in and trusted me. He did accept what I said. He did trust. And his life was saved. His rescue became a headline in a national newspaper.

The boy had to accept what I said and trust. And that is

exactly what Wisdom is saying to us, both in the verses for today and throughout the book of Proverbs. Accept, without question that what Wisdom is saying is true and jump into the waters of life, trusting and obeying. For, Wisdom says, *"I will instruct you in the way of wisdom and lead you along straight paths. When you walk, your steps will not be hampered; when you run, you will not stumble."*

This is extraordinarily good news – for these are the rich promises of God to His children. But in order to enjoy the promised blessings, we must *"hold on to instruction"*. We must not *"let it go"*. And we must *"guard it well"* for it is our life. If the boy in the river had not obeyed instruction I couldn't have saved him and he would have lost his life.

Your life is utterly precious. Jesus died that you might be forgiven and to give you a new, born-again, life. He has a destiny and a purpose for you. But Satan is a destiny-robber and he wants to entice you away from God's best and make you doubt the truth of God's Word and, even, rob you of your life. Follow the advice of Wisdom in the book of Proverbs and God's life-transforming keys will open the doors of opportunity for you. Today is the first day of the rest of your life. I pray that you will want to follow Him every step of the way.

Prayer: *Thank You, Jesus, for showing us that You are the way to life. Help me, Lord, to always follow the instruction of Wisdom and so enjoy the blessings You have promised in Your Word. I choose now to step into the destiny You have reserved for me by accepting all that You say as the truth and follow You all my days. In Jesus' Name, Amen.*

Personal Notes

Thank You Heavenly Father
for keeping me, my family
& all our loved ones as
well as colleagues in good
health, in Jesus Name.
May our Lives bring
glory to Your most Holy
Name now & always.
AMEN, AMEN and AMEN !!!

About the Author

Peter Horrobin is the Founder and International Director of Ellel Ministries International, which began in 1986 as a ministry of healing in the north-west of England. The work is now established in over thirty-five different countries.

After graduating from Oxford University with a degree in Chemistry, he spent a number of years in College and University lecturing, before leaving the academic environment for the world of business, where he founded a series of successful publishing and bookselling companies.

In his twenties he started to restore a vintage sports car (an *Alvis Speed 20*) but discovered that its chassis was bent. As he looked at the broken vehicle, wondering if it could ever be repaired, he sensed God asking him a question, *"You could restore this broken car, but I can restore broken lives. Which is more important?"* It was obvious that broken lives were more important than broken cars and so the beginnings of a vision for restoring people was birthed in his heart.

A hallmark of Peter's ministry has been his willingness to step out in faith and see God move to fulfil His promises, often in remarkable ways. His latest book, *Strands of Destiny*, is full of the stories of what God has done in the past thirty years.

Other books in this series

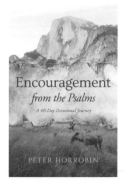

Encouragement from the Psalms
There are times in all our lives
when we need encouragement.
Encouragement enables us to look
up instead of down and gives us
the determination to keep going
whatever our circumstances. God
is a great encourager, as David
discovered throughout his years
of seeking to walk in God's ways.
These devotionals, which are built
around key verses in the Psalms, reflect on how God
encouraged David and provide daily encouragement for
Christian believers today.
144 pages, RRP £9.99
ISBN 978-1-85240-801-5
Available Autumn 2018

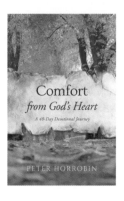

Comfort from God's Heart
Paul referred to God as *'the God of
ALL comfort'*. Meaning that whatever
our situation or circumstances God
wants to be our ultimate source
of comfort. And Jesus also said,
*"Blessed are those that mourn, for they
shall be comforted".* But it's not just
at times of mourning that we need
comfort. Life can deliver some hard
blows and unless we learn to turn

to God for the comfort we need, we may be tempted to find our comfort in all the wrong places. This devotional volume draws on many different parts of the Bible to deliver a message of comfort from the heart of God.

144 pages,
ISBN 978-1-85240-816-9
Available Spring 2019

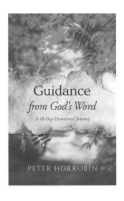

Guidance from God's Word

God has prepared a way ahead for each one of our lives and one of the prevailing cries of the human heart is for God's guidance along the path of life. Psalm 119 begins by saying *"Blessed are they whose ways are blameless, who walk according to the law of the Lord."* This very practical devotional volume sets out in forty faith-building steps the foundational principles of how God uses His Word to guide and direct us and show us how to know His will for our lives.

144 pages,
ISBN 978-1-85240-846-6
Available Summer 2019

Further books by Peter Horrobin

Strands of Destiny

Peter Horrobin's personal account of how God envisioned him through the remains of a crashed car, and then established the healing work of Ellel Ministries at Ellel Grange, will build your faith as you journey with him through the ups and downs of what became a world-wide spiritual adventure.

Paperback 464 pages plus 48 pages of colour photographs, £14.99, ISBN 978-1-85240-835-0

Healing Through Deliverance

In this comprehensive, practical and ground-breaking volume, Peter draws on this extensive experience to set out a thorough and scriptural foundation for the healing and deliverance ministry—an integral part of fulfilling the Great Commission and a vital key to discipleship. This authoritative handbook will equip you to understand and respond to the call of God to set the captives free. A classic.

Hardback 630 pages, £24.99, ISBN 978-1-852404-98-7

Healing from the consequences of Accident, Shock and Trauma

Unhealed trauma is one of the primary reasons why some people do not easily heal from the consequences of accidents or sudden shocks. This ground-breaking book is the culmination of thirty years of experience praying for such people. This foundational teaching has been instrumental in bringing permanent healing to people all over the world.

Paperback 176 pages, £9.99, ISBN 9781852407438

Forgiveness – God's Master Key

Forgiveness is key to the restoration of our relationship with God and to healing from the consequences of hurtful, damaging human relationships. This book is one of the most outstanding and concise available on the subject of forgiveness.

Paperback 110 pages, £6.99, ISBN 978-1-852405-02-1

Living Life God's Way

Peter Horrobin guides you through a landscape of hidden truths. Using real life testimonies, parables and illustrations to unlock some of the most difficult of life's issues that often make us stumble through our Christian walk.

Paperback 222 pages, £10.99, ISBN 978-1-85240-758-2

The Truth Stick

A Parable for Adults and Children

Ratty, Mole and Badger get caught up in life-changing adventures as they look for an answer to Ratty's big question, "What is truth?" A delightful, thought provoking story for the young in heart of all ages.

Hardback 128 pages, £9.99, ISBN 0-9546380-1-8

The Parables of Harris

Lessons from the Real-Life Adventures of a Black Labrador

From the founders of Ellel Ministries International, comes this amusing and entertaining book about Harris, a black Labrador belonging to the Horrobins, whose adventurous exploits have become modern-day parables, serving the reader with essential insights into life in general.

Paperback 128 pages, £6.99, ISBN 0-9546380-0-X

Journey to Freedom

This remarkable series of eight books by **Peter Horrobin**, *the Founder of Ellel Ministries*, is a life-transforming library which takes the reader one step at a time on a journey of personal transformation. Every book is packed with vital Bible-based teaching, insights and stories from Peter's thirty years of ministry experience. His relational style is easy to read. He explains difficult issues in ways that make them easy to understand. Many remarkable testimonies witness to the power of the Holy Spirit ministering healing life through the teaching.

"I weep with gratitude for what God has done for me" and *"This has changed my life for ever – the most fulfilling and exciting experience I have had in my walk with the Lord".*

Originally published over a twelve-month period, as a daily on-line journey called *Ellel 365*, **this outstanding teaching is now available in book-form for the very first time.** While each book is complete in itself, the reader is also invited to step out on their own journey of faith and understanding as they take daily steps of faith through all eight books in the series.

Book 1 **Building on the Rock** *Available in Autumn 2018*
Book 2 **God, Me and the Enemy** *Available in Autumn 2018*
Book 3 **Our Faithful God** *Available in Autumn 2018*

Book 4 **Jesus – Our Living Hope** *Available in Spring 2019*
Book 5 **Jesus – Healer and Deliverer** *Available in Spring 2019*
Book 6 **Dying to Live** *Available in Spring 2019*

Book 7 **God's Plan for My Healing** *Available in Autumn 2019*
Book 8 **My Life in God's Hands** *Available in Autumn 2019*

All these books and more are available from Sovereign World.

Sovereign World Ltd
Please visit our online shop to browse our range of titles.
www.sovereignworld.com
or write to the company at the headquarters address:

Sovereign World Ltd.
P.O.Box 784
Ellel
Lancaster
LA1 9DA
United Kingdom

Or email us at:
info@sovereignworld.com

Most books are also available in e-book format and can be purchased online.

Ellel Ministries
International

About Ellel Ministries

Our Vision

Ellel Ministries is a non-denominational Christian Mission Organization with a vision to resource and equip the Church by welcoming people, teaching them about the Kingdom of God and healing those in need (Luke 9:11).

Our Mission

Our mission is to fulfil the above vision throughout the world, as God opens the doors, in accordance with the Great Commission of Jesus and the calling of the Church to proclaim the Kingdom of God by preaching the good news, healing the broken-hearted and setting the captives free. We are, therefore, committed to evangelism, healing, deliverance, discipleship and training. The particular scriptures on which our mission is founded are Isaiah 61:1–7; Matthew 28:18–20; Luke 9:1–2; 9:11; Ephesians 4:12; 2 Timothy 2:2.

Our Basis of Faith

God is a Trinity. God the Father loves all people. God the Son, Jesus Christ, is Saviour and Healer, Lord and King. God the Holy Spirit indwells Christians and imparts the dynamic power by which they are enabled to continue Christ's ministry. The Bible is the divinely inspired authority in matters of faith, doctrine and conduct, and is the basis for teaching.

For details about the current worldwide activities of Ellel Ministries International please go to: www.ellel.org

Ellel Ministries International
Ellel Grange
Ellel
Lancaster, LA2 0HN
United Kingdom
Tel (+44) (0)1524 751 651

Would You Join With Us To Bless the Nations?

At the Sovereign World Trust, our mandate and passion is to send books, like the one you've just read, to *faithful leaders who can equip others* (2 Tim 2:2).

The 'Good News' is that in all of the poorest nations we reach, the Kingdom of God is growing in an accelerated way but, to further this Great Commission work, the Pastors and Leaders in these countries need good teaching resources in order to provide sound Biblical doctrine to their flock, their future generations and especially new converts.

If you could donate a copy of this or other titles from Sovereign World Ltd, you will be helping to supply much-needed resources to Pastors and Leaders in many countries.

Contact us for more information on (+44)(0)1732 851150 or visit our website www.sovereignworldtrust.org.uk

> *"I have all it takes to further my studies. Sovereign is making it all possible for me"*
>
> **Rev. Akfred Keyas – Kenya**

> *"My ministry is rising up gradually since I have been teaching people from these books"*
>
> **Pastor John Obaseki – Nigeria**